THE SLOYD SERIES

THE SLOYD SYSTEM OF WOOD WORKING

With A Brief Description Of
The Eva Rodhe Model Series And
An Historical Sketch Of
The Growth Of The Manual Training Idea

By

Benjamin B. Hoffman, A. B.

Superintendent Of
The Baron De Hirsch Fund Trade Schools

1892

Toolemera Press
History Preserved
toolemerapress.com

The Sloyd System Of Wood Working: With A Brief Description Of The Eva Rodhe Model Series And An Historical Sketch Of The Growth Of The Manual Training Idea
By Benjamin B. Hoffman, A. B.: Superintendent Of The Baron De Hirsch Fund Trade Schools
Originally published by The American Book Company
1892

Toolemera Press: The Sloyd Series

No part of this book may be reproduced, stored in an electronic retrieval system, or transmitted in any form or by an means, electronic, mechanical, photocopy, photographic or otherwise without the written permission of the publisher.

Excerpts of one page or less for the purposes of review and comment are permissible.

Copyright © 2020 Gary Roberts DBA Toolemera Press

International Standard Book Number
ISBN: 9781087863580
(Trade Paper)

Published by
Gary Roberts DBA, The Toolemera Press
Wilmington, North Carolina USA 28401
www.toolemerapress.com

Toolemera Press publishes The Sloyd Series, preserving in print classic books on the theories and applications of Sloyd.

- The Teacher's Hand-Book Of Slojd, by Otto Salomon ISBN: 9780983150091

- Sloyd In Great Britain And America 1890 & 1906. ISBN: 9781087806259

- The Sloyd System Of Wood Working, by Benjamin B. Hoffman. ISBN: 9781087863580

Period Reviews

The Teacher: February, 1893. Vol. VI; No. 1, page 198
The Sloyd System Of Wood-Working. By B. B Hoffman, Superintendent of the Baron De Hirsch Fund Trade Schools. New York: American Book Company.

We have here both the theory and the practice of the "Naas System" of manual training. The first chapter is devoted to "The Theory Of The Sloyd System Of Wood-Working" and all that this implies. The second chapter is devoted to special arrangements of the Sloyd. Chapter third is taken up with the history of manual-training and the development of the idea in Europe. This chapter includes Alfred Johannson's Naas Model Series and Otto Salomon's Indtroduction. Chapter fifth includes Eva Rothe's (sic) Model Series; and the last chapter treats of the "progress of the Sloyd in the elementary schools and the extension of the movement in Europe and America" The chapter of the history of manual training includes only an account of the movement in Europe. Is is to be regretted that a brief description of the movement in this country is not included. There is of course a great deal of literature on this subject already in the hands of the public, but we think this work would be improved if brief mention were made of the work of the Industrial Education Association (now the Teachers College), Dr. Belfield's Manual-Training School in Chicago, and the work of Professor C. M. Woodward in the St. Louis School and his efforts in general for the benefit of the cause of manual training in the United States. Of course there is a difference between Sloyd and manual training, and perhaps the author did not refer to the above because of his "Sloyd" view of manual training. The practical part of this book is a very valuable feature; and teachers, by carefully studying its (sic) directions, could get a working knowlege of Sloyd. Indeed aas regards this feature the little book is the very best of its kind.

The Journal Of Education: Vol. 37; No. 8 (908), February 23, 1893, page 123
The Sloyd System Of Wood Working. By B. B. Hoffman, A. B. New York: American Book Co. 242 pp. Price, $1.00

This is a curiosity bordering on fascination to see the entire school room literature upon a given subject spring into being, each leading house bringing out a work of special merit. The subjects of physiology, music, drawing, biology, gymnastics, furnish admirable illustrations of the growth of a literature.

With the incoming of books upon a new subject, it is interesting to see how each emphasizes what has been hitherto unemphasized. In the case of an old subject like arithmetic, in connection with which conservative prejudices are strong, no publisher quite dares to break away from traditions.

In the matter of manual training, the great battle to be fought is whether of not America is to use sloyd; i.e., the sloyd of Naas as expounded by Otto Salomon and A. Sluys, or whether there is to be an Americanized sloyd after the style of Woodward or some other skilled American enthusiast. This volume presents in an admirable manner the Swedish system in all its attractiveness. It is Americanized in this only that it is made "workable" at every point. There has been no ingenious presentation of a modified or Americanized sloyd that was more usable than this purely classical presentation of the Swedish work. There is, to many, a genuine satisfaction in dealing at first hand with a master, as one may do with the sloyd of Naas, in this text-book, which is more than a handbook - almost a treatise.

Economy In Education: A Practical Discussion Of Present Day Problems In Educational Administration. R. N Roark. 1905

Hoffman's Sloyd System Of Wood-Working by B. B. Hoffman, A. B., formerly Superintendent of the Baron De Hirsch Fund Trade Schools. . . .$1.00

The object of this book is to give an account of the theory and practical application of the "Sloyd System" of manual training. It also includes a list and drawings of the models of the "Rodhe System" for children of the age of five to eleven years, filling the void between the kindergarten and the Sloyd system. In the treatment of the practical work, as few technical expressions as possible have been used, so that a teacher who may have had no previous experience in work of this kind may nevertheless be able to follow out a course of manual training in wood work without any outside assistance.

www.toolemerapress.com

Gary Roberts, publisher of the Toolemera Press imprint, preserves in print classic books on early crafts, trades and industries. All titles are produced from the originals in his personal collection.

THE SLOYD SYSTEM

OF

WOOD WORKING

WITH A BRIEF DESCRIPTION OF THE EVA RODHE MODEL SERIES
AND AN HISTORICAL SKETCH OF THE GROWTH
OF THE MANUAL TRAINING IDEA

BY

B. B. HOFFMAN, A.B.
SUPERINTENDENT OF THE BARON DE HIRSCH FUND TRADE SCHOOLS

NEW YORK ·:· CINCINNATI ·:· CHICAGO
AMERICAN BOOK COMPANY

COPYRIGHT, 1892, BY
AMERICAN BOOK COMPANY.
W. P. 1

PREFACE.

THE object of this book is to give an account of the theory and practical application of the "Nääs System" of manual training. Although the principles upon which this system has been founded are very fully explained in the two educational monographs of the New York College for the Training of Teachers, entitled "The Sloyd in the Service of the School," by Otto Salamon, and "Manual Training in Elementary Schools for Boys," by A. Sluys, a full exposition of the subject as taught in the Nääs Sloyd Seminarium, and as incorporated in the Swedish public schools, has not as yet appeared. The author hopes that the following chapters may in a measure supply this want.

In the chapter on the practical work, as few technical expressions as possible have been used, so that a teacher who may have had no previous experience in work of this kind may nevertheless be able to follow out a course of manual training in wood-work without any outside assistance.

Chapter III. is a translation of Book V. of Director Otto Salamon's "Sloyd och Folkskola" ("Sloyd and the Public School"), which gives an account of the history of the manual training idea. Chapter VI. is a translation of Mr. Salamon's article on Sloyd in the "Nordeska Familie Bok" ("Northern Encyclopedia").

The book also includes a list and drawings of the models of the Eva Rodhe System for children of the age of five to eleven years. In the "Pratiska Arbetskolan" ("Practical Working School") in Gothenburg, this system has been taught for a number of years, and has met with considerable success, filling the void between the Kindergarten and the "Nääs System."

The author desires to express his sincere thanks to Director Otto Salamon, Mr. Alfred Johannson, Mr. Jacob Hyberg of Nääs, Sweden, and to Mr. George E. Tuthill of New York, for valuable assistance in the preparation of this work.

CONTENTS.

Chapter	Page
I. The Theory of the Sloyd System of Wood-Working	9
The Need for Manual Training	9
Various Systems of Manual Training	12
A Love for Work	23
Respect for Rough Bodily Labor	25
Self-reliance and Independence	26
Order and Exactness	28
Attention	29
Industry and Perseverance	30
Physical Power	31
The Chest, Head, and Feet	34
Position in Sawing and Planing	35
To Train the Eye to the Sense of Form	36
General Dexterity of Hand	36
II. Special Arrangements of the Sloyd	39
Many Forms of Manual Work	39
Arrangement of the Models	44
Tools	45
Age of Pupils, Length of Lessons, etc.	46
Who shall be the Teacher	47
Individual and Class Teaching	48

CONTENTS

CHAPTER	PAGE
III. The History of Manual Training	53
Development of the Idea in Europe	53
IV. Alfred Johannson's Nääs Model Series	91
Otto Salamon's Introduction	91
The Nääs Models	96
Fundamental Series	101
Town Elementary Series	191
High School Series	201
V. Eva Rodhe's Model Series	219
Introduction	219
The Eva Rodhe Models	223
VI. The Progress of the Sloyd in the Elementary Schools	235
Extension of the Movement in Europe and America	235

CHAPTER I.

THE THEORY OF THE SLOYD SYSTEM OF WOOD-WORKING.

THE NEED FOR MANUAL TRAINING.

THAT book-training alone is not sufficient to educate the child is shown by the fact that during the past twenty years, throughout both Europe and America, various systems of handicraft work have been introduced in the schools as part of the elementary school instruction, educators and teachers in all countries having found something lacking in the ordinary form of public education.

They saw that the youth, who, after leaving the school, started out to make his own living, was in many cases quite unable to do so, and naturally the question arose: " Is the present form of public education of a nature calculated to fit the child for a useful career in life? If not, what reforms can be instituted so that the school instruction will be better able to meet the exigencies of life and the demands of the times?"

In all educational circles these questions have been discussed; and, as a direct result, we find that different systems of manual training have been applied as remedies.

The chief arguments, and those which have greatly influenced the adoption of some of the present European systems of manual training, are the so-called "Economic" and the "Educational" arguments.

On the one hand, the "Educational" advocates urged that in order to systematically develop the natural forces it was necessary, from a psychological point of view, to try to give to the child the ability to express objects by means of delineation and construction, and thus to add to the power of mere verbal description. In other words, "It is more natural for the boy to be able to draw a sphere, or to make one out of wood or clay, than to understand the geometrical definition of a sphere."

On the other hand, the "Economic" argument was based more particularly upon the social and industrial benefits to be derived from the training.

To the "Economic" argument was added the "Physiological." The researches of Hughlings,

Jackson, and Ferrier were frequently quoted. Their experiments proved that the brain is not, as was formerly supposed, a single organ acting as a whole, but a congeries of organs capable of more or less independent action.

In speaking of these experiments, and their connection with early manual education, a recent writer says: "As the development of the motor centers in the brain hinges, in a great degree, upon the movements and exercises of youth, it will be readily understood how important is the nature of the part played by the early exercise of the hand in evoking inherited skill and in creating the industrial capabilities of a nation.

"There can be no doubt that the most active epoch in the development of these motor centers is from the fourth to the fifteenth year, after which they become comparatively fixed and stubborn. Hence it can be understood that boys and girls whose hands have been left altogether untrained up to the fifteenth year are practically incapable of high manual efficiency thereafter."

The "Economic" advocates stated, furthermore, that by cramming the children's heads full of book-studies, and by withholding from them the exercise of their hands, the skill of a future race of mechanics was being destroyed.

VARIOUS SYSTEMS OF MANUAL TRAINING.

Of the various systems of manual training that have been introduced in the elementary public schools of Europe, the *Della Vos* in Russia, the *Salicis* in France, and the *Sloyd* in Sweden, Norway, Denmark, Finland, and recently in special schools in England, Germany, Belgium, and Italy, are the most prominent.

The French system, under the name of *L'enseignement du Travail Manuel*, was made compulsory in the public schools in 1882.

It was mainly due to the efforts of M. Buisson, Director of Primary Instruction, that in this year a special normal school was created in France, in which wood-working at the bench and lathe, iron-working in the smithery, with vise and turning-lathe, drawing, modeling, molding, and graphic designing were the principal subjects of instruction. Experimental physics, chemistry, natural history, fencing, and fire-practice were likewise taught.

This institution was founded after a vote had been taken in the Chamber of Deputies, in March of 1882. Admission was granted by competition to forty-eight school-teachers, graduates of the Université de France. It was a one-year course. To-day we find that each year about fifteen hundred students are being graduated from the various normal schools in France.

"In fifteen years," said the late Inspector-General A. Salicis, "nearly all our primary high schools, and most of our forty thousand elementary schools for boys ought to provide our 2,750,000 male children of the working classes with the instruction which will fit them for the future they have in store. If we do not speak of the girls, it is because they have already, to a certain extent, a suitable primary course in manual training, consisting of needlework, cutting out, and dressmaking."

The object of this system is clearly expressed in the words of the French minister of public instruction : "The love for work can only come through the habit of working; and, reciprocally, the habit of work can only come by implanting the love for it."

In short, from this early acquired taste should be engendered a precocious ability—an indispensable condition of future excellency, and consequently a condition of economic success in foreign markets.

In 1868 a systematic method of teaching the arts of turning, carpentering, fitting, and forging was introduced in the Imperial School at Moscow, under the directorship of Victor Della Vos. These arts were taught because they were considered to be the foundation of all mechanical pursuits.

Furthermore, the school council, who inaugurated this system, found it necessary to separate the school shops from the mechanical works, admitting pupils to the latter only when they had perfectly acquired the principles of practical labor. This was done in order to secure a symmetrical teaching of elementary practical work, as well as for the more convenient supervision of the pupils while practically employed. It is the first known instance of such an arrangement.

The primary object of the Russian method was to teach the child manual work, if not directly for the purpose of fitting him for a future vocation in the arts or trades, at least in order to make him more capable, in case he should select some mechanical pursuit as his future work in life.

Since 1872 the study of the Sloyd in the Folkskola (public school) of Sweden has created the most intense interest. The Sloyd, a system of manual training in wood and metal work, is taught as an optional study in fifteen hundred schools in Sweden to boys of the age of ten to fourteen years.

At the present time, the *Nääs System*, arranged by Otto Salamon, director of the Nääs Normal College, has been universally adopted. This has been called the *Sloyd System*. Its object is solely educational. The faults of the old method of teaching only theoretical subjects being recognized, the best ideas of the teachers in this field were studied, and a method was formulated which combines hand and head work in the simplest way possible.

The word *system* is meant to convey the idea of a plan running through the work, which rests on a scientific basis and holds good for those classes for which it is intended.

In speaking of the Sloyd System, it is necessary not to confound the Sloyd series of models with the system itself. The two are entirely distinct. A series of models is never more than the outward expression of an idea. Models of almost any kind could be constructed upon the principles that underlie those of the Nääs series, and, though very different in form, they might have equal educational advantages, and might even be more applicable in certain instances. It is from the point of view of the system that the models should be judged.

The word *Sloyd* (Swedish, *Slöjd*) is derived from the Icelandic, and means dexterity or skill. In old Swedish, we find the adjective *slög* (artistic or skillful). In the Low German dialect, the word *Klütern* has a similar signification. There is in Sweden a distinct class of workmen known as *Sloyders*, whom we would call "jacks of all trades," as they are able to do various kinds of odd jobs about a house. The Swedish word *Slöjd* exists in other languages, but has a more restricted meaning, referring to the educational idea. In English it is synonymous with *manual training* as distinct from technical and industrial training.

The problem which confronted the educators was how to create a manual training system which would be a true factor in public education. Public education is designed to be a systematic influence for the good, exercised by the teacher upon the minds and characters of the pupils; it aims to make them more fit to cope with the difficulties of life, and thus to make them useful and honorable members of the community. Would manual training be of material aid in this direction?

The immediate object of all public education being thus defined, teachers came to the conclusion that the instruction should be imparted not only for the sake of the actual knowledge to be derived, most of which must of necessity in time be forgotten, but principally as a means of developing the character.

At one time it was thought best to allow the home influence to be the sole guide in the formation of character, but the error of such a course became evident when it was considered that it was impossible to determine whether the home influence would be exerted for the good or for the evil. Again, the duties of the parents were found at times to be of such a nature as to prevent their giving the proper attention to the education of their children.

It was therefore decided that the work of elevating each life should be carried on in the school, where the child is competing all the time for some desired goal, and consequently soon begins to feel the necessity of knowing and doing.

He feels this in the school even more than in the home; for the school is to the child like a little world, which has much in common with the larger one for which he is preparing himself. It therefore becomes the duty of the school to train the heart, the mind, and the body harmoniously.

Since the work of the school is so important, and since the entire school life of most children must be limited to a period of from six to eight years, it seemed desirable that the school should arrange its course of study and its methods of instruction in such a way that each subject would be a means of educational development. Any subject which did not fulfill this requirement was not to be taught. No subject was to be taught simply for the sake of imparting information.

By experiment it was found that manual work tended to develop character, mind, and body, and that it gave such information as was necessary and useful after the school period was passed, increasing in each individual the capacity for work. It was therefore decided that it should hold a place among the school studies.

We must now distinguish between the general object of all systems of manual training, and the special purposes to be served by the system here under consideration.

The object of introducing manual training into the public schools is well defined by Prof. C. M. Woodward, when he says: " We do not wish to make mechanics. We teach banking, not because we expect our pupils to become bankers; we teach drawing, not because we expect to train architects, artists, or engineers; and we teach the use of tools, the properties of materials, and the methods of the arts, not because we expect our boys to become artisans. We teach them the United States Constitution and some of the Acts of Congress, not because we expect them all to become congressmen. But we *do* expect that our boys will, at least, have something to do with bankers, and architects, and artists, and engineers, and artisans; and we *do* expect all to become good citizens. Our great object is educational; other objects are secondary."

The Sloyd has for its first object* to give an indirect preparation for life by teaching branches of certain trades and by imparting a general dexterity to the hand—to train the hand as the obedient servant of the brain.

The Swedes set out to accomplish this by teaching the boys in the schools the rudiments of special trades; they discarded that system some years ago, adopting the present one in its stead.

---

* These are the aims of the Sloyd instruction as set forth by Director Otto Salamon in his lectures. It will of course be understood that any statement of results to be achieved must in a great measure be conditional; yet the object of the work, and the probable effects, must surely be best known to him who has arranged the course, and who has daily watched its effects upon the minds and characters of many hundreds of children.

Experience taught them that the boy was not old enough to know what particular trade he should choose. Again, usually only one trade could be taught, and this, of course, did not accomplish the aim with which the instruction was given. From a practical point of view, any one of the important trades is as necessary as the other.

It was impossible to teach any one trade thoroughly in so short a time as could be devoted to it at school; and, as a result, many children left the school impressed with the false notion that they were competent workmen. How fatal such a spirit was, need hardly be stated.

The second object of the Sloyd is to develop the mental faculties, and at the same time to impart positive useful information. As Froebel had provided a system which gave expression to this idea by creating the kindergarten, and as he had felt that this was a principle which would regulate every step in the child's education, so it is to this end, also, that the Sloyd aims.

It embraces the doctrine which educators and teachers have been preaching for a long time—that of giving a practical direction to mental activity. Man is not only born to think, but also to do. He is a creative animal; he can and must embody his ideas in form.

The third object of the Sloyd is to make it a means of intensifying intuitions, thereby giving a clearer insight into the nature of things. As Herbart desired to see instruction more concentrated, all the subjects closely interwoven, the one serving to aid in the comprehension of the other—so the Sloyd, in combining the theoretical and practical, by teaching the elements of the arts and sciences, and the method of construction and illustration, aims to excite the intuitive faculty.

It is hardly likely that the efforts of a child will be adequate to provide accurate scientific apparatus to be used in the class-room, but the making of objects directly connected with the theoretical studies will increase the interest in the work and excite new ideas.

Sloyd aims to cultivate dexterity in the manipulation of tools. This is considered as one of its secondary aims. Too much stress must not be laid upon the use of tools, as the pupil is apt to lose interest in the work if he does not see a full and quick result for his labor.

In France, at one time, the children were taught various exercises in the use of tools, and models were not made at all. In the Danish system, the making of models is considered of quite secondary importance. Very few are made, and these only because they necessitate certain useful exercises of the tools. The use of many tools should be taught, but should serve rather as a means than an end to this instruction.

Primarily Sloyd is to be used as a means of *formal education*—formal as opposed to material. A material education seeks to impart a definite knowledge of things for their own sake. A formal education seeks chiefly to develop the innate mental powers, and selects and imparts knowledge in order to strengthen character, will-power, memory, perception—in short, all of those faculties of the mind which at birth are dormant, and which gradually and through education become to a greater or lesser degree marked characteristics of the individual.

All subjects can be used both for material and formal instruction—some more, some less. History and science give material information; and yet, if the teacher seeks to arouse the imaginative faculty, or to inspire a love and sympathy for humanity, a formal training is thereby added. The child when he studies his history lessons sees that among the first causes of a nation's welfare may be traced the underlying principle of order. Again, as he becomes acquainted with the elements of the sciences, and as he begins to understand the workings of nature's laws, a desire to systematize and arrange things in a rational and orderly manner takes possession of his mind. Mathematics and gymnastics are of more value as formal than as material means of education, as the former develops the reasoning faculty, while the latter strengthens the body. Materialists believe in giving a knowledge of the actual things met with in life, while the formalists lay stress upon the cultivation of correct habits.

Sloyd has for its aims, as a means of formal instruction—to instil a love for work in general; to create a respect for rough, honest bodily labor; to develop self-reliance and independence; to train to habits of order, exactness, cleanliness, and neatness; to teach habits of attention, industry, and perseverance; to promote the development of the physical powers; to train the eye to the sense of form, and to cultivate the dexterity of the hand.

A LOVE FOR WORK.

No child can enjoy a healthy happiness without doing some work. Most children are inquisitive, and want to know facts about the objects they see and handle. As an infant, the child constantly moves, and grasps at everything that he sees; and, as he grows older, he shows similar impulses in his delight in building, constructing, and destroying objects.

In order to bring about a love for work, it is necessary that the work be useful, otherwise it will soon become tiresome. The work should not require wearisome preparatory exercises; this is apt to cause the distaste which we have often seen among apprentices to the various trades. The work must afford variety—not necessarily novelty, but there must be a change, and not too much of one thing at a time.

The children must be capable of doing the entire work themselves, for they feel happy only when they can feel and say that they have done it all themselves. The teacher must refrain from forcing a child to accept much unnecessary assistance. To help the child to overcome all the difficulties which will necessarily arise, and then to permit him to claim the work as his own, encourages him to deceive others, and, worse than that, leads him to deceive himself.

The work must be real, and not "play at work." If the occupation has no serious importance, but is merely given to keep the children busy and out of mischief, the true educational value is lost.

Finally, the work, when finished, must become the property of the child, for he has purchased the right to it with his own labor.

From the outset, the child must be shown the true nature of the work, so that he will do it voluntarily and in a proper spirit. M. Pizzurno translates from an Italian pamphlet into French the following passage: "It is not possible to produce in facsimile a pattern of every article we make; but it is important that a thing be done as accurately as possible from the outset, and the earlier we teach the child this, the better it will be in the end."

RESPECT FOR ROUGH BODILY LABOR.

We no longer absolutely despise hard bodily labor as we did a century ago, when to do nothing was considered more honorable than to work; yet even to-day we attach a certain stigma of inferiority to all forms of bodily labor. In the social world, the clerk ranks higher than the skilled artisan, and the workmen themselves are only too apt to consider that their labor is less honorable than that of their masters.

This perverted idea may be a survival of the opinion that prevailed in the middle ages, when all rough work was done by serfs. The labor question is one of the important problems of our times. We know that there are many causes at work which sow discord between capitalists and laborers. Would it not be a step taken in the right direction if each child in the rising generation could be inspired with a true respect for rough physical labor, so that as workman he could find contentment in his vocation, and as capitalist he would not undervalue the true worth of his artisans? We cannot make children respect rough labor unless we let them take part in it themselves.

To inspire the child with a respect for rough labor, the models produced must not be fancy knick-knacks or articles of luxury. If taught only to do fancy and decoration work, he may be inclined to regard rougher forms of labor as of inferior dignity.

SELF-RELIANCE AND INDEPENDENCE.

It is of the utmost importance that we help the child to utilize that which he knows, and force him to give some visible expression and some practical application to the information he has acquired. Here is one of the teacher's most difficult tasks. There are many people possessed

SELF-RELIANCE AND INDEPENDENCE 27

of much knowledge, who totally lack the power of applying it.

Home lessons are intended to test the children's power of working alone, but they often fail to accomplish this object, because some parents allow their children to neglect their home work, while others provide private teachers. Even in the class-room, it is often difficult to get clear answers without occasionally prompting and helping the children.

By means of the Sloyd, however, it is very easy for the teacher to set a certain task to be performed, and to detect and prevent any undue assistance.

Self-reliance can best be encouraged if the work is adapted to the capabilities of the pupil; that is, it must be neither too easy nor too difficult. If it is too easy, no real development is insured; if too difficult, dependence upon others must result.

The teacher should conduct, control, and superintend the work, but must guard against putting his hand to it. Nothing is gained by getting the child to produce a faultless model if this is not the result of his own unaided exertion.

The child must use his judgment at every step, must recognize that he, and not the teacher, is responsible for the work. This is the only way in which independence can be fostered.

If necessary, the teacher should illustrate on a different piece of wood. The rule, "Never touch the child's model," has no exception.

In order to sustain the interest in the work, the child should never be compelled to make the same model more than twice in succession.

ORDER AND EXACTNESS.

The habits of order and exactness, which appear to be contrary to the natural instincts of many children, require much training. Order refers to an absolute idea; exactness is more relative. It is quite possible to make very exact models, and yet remain very disorderly in the manner of work. These habits are, in a sense, the foundation of an æsthetic education.

Disorderly habits and inexactness are always antagonistic to a true conception of beauty. Much has been said about giving the young an æsthetic education; but it seems that the real foundation for this instruction has been neglected, inasmuch as stress has been laid upon the decoration of objects before the objects were correctly made. As a result, we find that many children think certain objects beautiful, which are in reality only highly ornamented. The child must be taught from the very beginning to understand form as well as decoration.

No matter how useful a dirty or repulsive work may be, it is not suitable to be taught in the schools. The models must always be of such a nature and material that they will admit of being copied with order, exactness, neatness, and cleanliness.

ATTENTION.

A teacher's work is useless if the child is inattentive. Many discussions have centered upon the time to be devoted to certain subjects, but the question as to *how* a subject can be taught so as to attract and fix the attention is worthy of greater consideration; for more matter can often be taught in half an hour, if it is rightly presented, than in an hour, if it fails to attract the attention of the pupils. It has been said, with some truth, that if we work six hours a day, we do six hours' work; whereas if we work eight hours, we do but four hours' work.

In order to attract the attention, the chief thing necessary is to bring about a true and not a specious interest. The former consists in a desire to understand the subject for its own sake; the latter, for the sake of marks or rewards. In teaching theoretical subjects, it is at times very difficult to know whether the attention of a child is fixed or not. He may appear attentive, and yet his mind may be far away.

In the manual work, the pupil's attention is attracted in three different directions—on what the teacher says, for the pupil soon finds that he cannot do his work without attending very closely to instructions; upon himself, for otherwise the child comes to grief with his tools; and upon the work engaged on, or he spoils it.

At Nääs, experience has shown that grown people destroy more work and hurt themselves more frequently than children. This is due to the fact that they have more to think about, and cannot concentrate their thoughts so fully upon any one particular object.

Here it is that the great value of all educational manual work shows itself—in cultivating the habit of attention. In order to create a habit of attention, the work must require mechanical as well as mental effort.

INDUSTRY AND PERSEVERANCE.

In the theoretical subjects the connection between industry and success is not apparent. It is often difficult to impress upon the child's mind the fact of his inability to execute any real work without industry and perseverance. If book studies alone are relied upon to bring this truth home, the task of the teacher becomes all the more ungrateful, because many children find it impossible to grasp theoretical studies. They do their best, and yet they fail.

The marking system is by no means a standard which will impress the child with an idea of the close relation existing between industry and success. Questions may be given which the child can answer correctly, though he himself feels that he has not comprehended the lesson. In manual work, however, industry can never fail to secure success.

The school life and the after school life have heretofore differed much in the demands they have made upon us. Society requires that men put their ideas into execution. Has the school heretofore desired the same? It may be said that a combination of manual and theoretical work reconciles the demands of the school with those of the world.

PHYSICAL POWER.

The ancients, and especially the Greeks, with their love of beauty and harmony, devoted much time to the symmetrical development of the human body. No nation since their time has attained so high a standard of physical strength combined with physical beauty.

In the middle ages we find two extremes—the monks, who mortified and suppressed every power of the body; and the knights, who performed prodigies of strength and agility, while their minds were often as empty as were their helmets.

In comparatively modern times, the education of the masses was confined chiefly to the mind, as no organized provision existed for the training of the body.

To-day this question is regarded from a scientific standpoint. It is recognized that the school work must include nothing which interferes with healthy bodily development.

In order to strengthen the body, the work must demand much movement, thereby counteracting the bad effects of sitting still in the class-room. The principles which underlie any rational system of gymnastics should guide us in this work.

Every exercise should have its appropriate position, which should be clearly explained. It may be argued that this is unnecessary, as each form of work instinctively suggests the most natural attitude; but the fallacy of such an argument is shown by the great mortality among men engaged in certain handicrafts, which is due to the cramped and unhealthy positions assumed in their occupations. Consumption, swelling of the veins and arteries, heart failure, and many other diseases are brought on by crowding the chest and by working with bent head.

Dr. B. W. Richardson, in his popular work on "Health and Occupation," has given much valuable information on this subject. It is quite natural for workmen to assume that position which will enable them to finish their tasks in the shortest period of time.

Knowing the evil effects of such habits, the teacher should be careful that the child does not assume a cramped position.

Another point to which attention should be directed is the equal exercise of both sides of the body. It still remains to be proven that the left side is *naturally* weaker than the right. There are many exercises which involve the use of both the right and the left sides, such as rowing, swimming, boxing, weaving, plowing, kneading, digging, driving, etc., and if the left appears the weaker, it is probably due to years of unsymmetrical training.

Special consideration should be given to the positions taken by the chest, head, and feet.

THE CHEST, HEAD, AND FEET.

It is of the greatest importance that the *chest* be permitted to expand freely. All prolonged work should be executed with the chest out and the shoulders thrown back. Contracted chests produce shortness of breath and palpitation of the heart.

The *head* should be held as erect as possible. By keeping the head in a bent position, the passage of the blood through the veins of the neck and throat is impeded (the vein tube being stretched vertically), and at the same time the muscles at the back of the neck, which hold up the head, become strained. When we are erect, much of the weight of the head is supported by the spine.

Again, in this bent position we look at objects from a wrong angle, and thus strain and injure the eyes. The work should be held at a distance of about thirty centimeters (one foot) from the eye.

In order that a worker may assume a firm and stable position, the direction of the resistance must at all times be taken into consideration. If the resistance comes from the front, one *foot* must be placed before the other, for the resistance offered must be as great a distance as possible from the center of gravity.

POSITION IN SAWING AND PLANING.

In *sawing*, it is thought best by some that the feet be placed at an angle of 90°; by others, at 60°. We consider 90° the better position. The shoulder and arm must be in line with the direction which the saw is to take. In order that the head may be held high and the chest well expanded, the benches should be so made that they can be raised or lowered as the work may require.

When sawing with the right arm, the left foot should be put straight out and parallel with the bench. When sawing with the left arm, the right foot should be put forward. The arm should move in the direction of the resistance. The saw should move in a line parallel with the bench. The body should move slowly backward and forward, and its swing should be regulated by the amount of resistance to be overcome.

In *planing*, the knee should be parallel to the bench, and one foot should be at right angles to the other. The pressure on the plane, so that the plane-iron will catch the wood, should come from the weight of the body. Very little force should be put upon the plane with the arms.

In drilling, the weight of the body should be used to overcome the resistance, since the pressure must be vertically downward.

TO TRAIN THE EYE TO THE SENSE OF FORM.

A number of models have been included in the Sloyd which might justly be termed "sense of form" models. Such models are principally those which are bounded by curved and regular surfaces in such a way that their general effect is pleasing to the eye.

As drawing trains the eye to a sense of outline, and modeling to a sense of solid form, so the manual wood-work should combine the two aims. In drawing we cannot exercise the sense of form to the greatest possible extent, as we have but a plane surface on which to represent that which we see. An important requisite is that all the models be artistic in form.

GENERAL DEXTERITY OF HAND.

A general dexterity of hand can only result from the education of many powers of the hands. It is not special dexterity, such as we see in mechanics or factory employes, though it always facilitates the acquirement of special dexterity. Sir Charles Bell in his treatise "On the Hand," gives us an excellent idea of its infinite uses.

The following are a few interesting examples of the great extent to which hand dexterity may be developed:

1. Two hundred and twenty-one words were written on a grain of wheat.
2. A Polish monk wrote the whole of the Iliad on a piece of paper that could be put into a nut-shell.
3. A Swede, Nauringaros, gave Pope Paul the Fifth twelve plates of ivory which were so small that they fitted inside of a pepper-corn.
4. A gold chain of fifty links, which could only be seen when placed on white paper, was presented to Queen Elizabeth.

These, then, are the aims of the Sloyd, as a means of *formal* education, while the *material* element may be considered to have been provided for in the power imparted of manipulating tools and of producing models. The real worth of the instruction is naturally something more than the making of any series of models. From a monetary point of view, much unnecessary time and labor are expended upon the models, but it is not correct to judge an educational system solely from a monetary point of view.

There are many ways in which Sloyd can be taught. It may be done with a view to economy, to utility, or as a ready-made plan of corporal work ; but the true way to bring about a lasting benefit is to regard it altogether as a means of education, and to attend to the teaching of its most minute details with this thought ever uppermost in the mind.

CHAPTER II.

SPECIAL ARRANGEMENTS OF THE SLOYD.

MANY FORMS OF MANUAL WORK.

THE simultaneous employment of many forms of manual training in the public schools is for several reasons detrimental to progress. A sufficient number of subjects is already being taught, and every branch of manual training is a distinct subject in itself. If the same advantages can be derived from one form of this work as from several forms, it is obviously better, on grounds of economy of time, labor, and expense, to confine the teaching to one.

When many kinds of manual training are undertaken at once, proficiency cannot be attained in any of them in the limited time devoted to each, the interest of the children is diverted, and in the end the true value is lost. If, however, we restrict the teaching to one particular kind of manual work, it is necessary that great caution be observed in choosing the best.

The various handicrafts have been subjected to the same tests, with the results shown in the table on p. 41. The following ten points have been considered:

1. Is the work in accordance with the average child's capabilities?
2. Does it excite and sustain interest? That is, after the novelty has worn off, does the interest flag or increase with each lesson?
3. Are the models of such a nature that they can be used? Are they as serviceable as an artisan's work, even though they are not as correctly finished?
4. Does the work tend to cultivate a respect for rough bodily labor?
5. Does it train to habits of order and exactness?
6. Is it of a character that admits of habits of cleanliness and neatness?
7. Does it cultivate the sense of form?
8. Is it beneficial from the hygienic point of view? Does it counteract the evil effects of sitting still?
9. Does it allow of methodical arrangement? Can the exercises be so arranged as to enable the pupil to proceed from the easy to the difficult, from the simple to the complex, so that at the beginning the work does not discourage him by its difficulty?
10. Does it teach general dexterity of hand?

It will be seen from the table that the carpentry Sloyd answers all of these questions in the affirmative.

THE ADVANTAGES OF THE VARIOUS FORMS OF MANUAL WORK.

MANY FORMS OF MANUAL WORK

	Is it in accordance with the child's capabilities?	Does it excite and sustain interest?	Are the objects made useful?	Does it give a respect for rough bodily labor?	Does it train to habits of order and exactness?	Does it allow of cleanliness and neatness?	Does it cultivate the sense of form?	Is it beneficial from the hygienic point of view?	Does it allow of methodical arrangement?	Does it teach general dexterity of hand?
Simple metal-work	Yes & No	Yes	Yes	Yes	Yes & No	Tolerably—No	Yes	Yes	Yes	Yes
Smith's work	No	Hardly	Tolerably	Yes	No	No	No?	Yes & No	Perhaps	No
Basket-making	No	Hardly	Tolerably	Yes	No	Yes?	No	No	No	No
Straw-plaiting	Yes	Yes?	Yes	Yes & No	Yes	No & Yes	No?	No	Yes	No
Brush-making	No?	Yes?	Yes & No	Yes?	Tolerably	No	No	No	No	No
House-painting	No	No	No & Yes	Yes	No	No	No	No	No	No
Fret-work	Yes?	No & Yes	No & Yes	No	Yes	Yes	No & Yes	No	No & Yes	No
Book-binding	No	No & Yes	Yes—Tolerably	Hardly	Tolerably	Yes?	No?	No	Perhaps	Tolerably
Card-board work	Yes & No	Yes?	Yes	No	Yes	Yes	Yes	Yes	Yes	No?
Sloyd carpentry	Yes	Yes	Yes	Yes	Yes	Yes	Yes	No	Yes	Yes
Sloyd wood-turning	No	Yes	Yes	Hardly	Partly	Yes	Yes	No	No	Yes
Sloyd wood-carving	Yes	Yes & No	Yes & No	No	Yes	Yes?	Yes & No	No	Yes	No
Modeling in clay	Yes	Yes	No	No	Yes & No	No	Yes	No	Yes	No

A marked difference exists between carpentry Sloyd (manual wood-work) and trade carpentry, as regards the character of the objects made.

In the former the objects are generally smaller; and as to the tools used, the carpenter has special planes, while in the Sloyd the knife is the essential tool, in place of which the carpenter uses the chisel.

The ax, bench-knife, and spoon-iron (which, though not carpenters' tools, are used by builders, wheelwrights, and coopers) are also used in the Sloyd.

Finally, there is a difference in the manner in which the work is done. In the trade carpentry there is a division of labor. In the Sloyd the complete object is made by one person.

With the Sloyd, wood-carving and wood-turning may be combined. The teacher may include both in the manual instruction, provided they do not prove too difficult.

When wood-carving is included in the course of instruction, great care must be taken that the objects to be carved are themselves correctly finished, as ornament should never conceal imperfect work.

The following are the principles which have served as guides in the *choice of the models*.

1. All articles of luxury have been excluded.

2. The objects have a practical value; that is, they can be used.

3. The objects can be finished by the pupils themselves without any help.

4. The objects are such that they can be made entirely of wood. This does not mean that the requisite fixings, such as screws, hangers, hinges, etc., may not be employed, but that the child should not be required to make these things.

5. The work is not to be polished. This refers to the use of clear-varnishes, French polish, etc.; sand-paper may be used. The object is to encourage the children to work well, and not to think too much of the surface appearance.

6. As little material as possible is to be used. The lesson to be enforced is that the value of the model depends not upon the material used, but upon the amount of real work expended upon it.

7. The pupils are to learn to work both in hard and soft wood. It is not wise to have them work too much in the hardest kinds of wood, as it is a great strain upon their physical strength, and consequently would soon prove beyond their powers.

8. Turning and carving are to be used as little as possible, although both may be included. Experience has shown that they are not as valuable as the carpentry Sloyd. The time for manual work in the public school is of necessity limited, and to teach turning and carving for educational purposes would require as much time as is necessary for the Sloyd. Carving in all cases ought to be left for the end of the course.

9. The models must develop the pupils' sense of form and beauty. In order to attain this object the series should in-

clude a number of examples of form, such as spoons, ladles, and other curved objects.

10. The whole series must be arranged so as to teach the pupils the use of all the necessary tools, and to know and perform the most important manipulations connected with wood-work. Each model ought to complete the preceding ones, and to teach the use of some new tool or some new kind of wood. The models constitute a series only when there is a logical connection between all of them, each one being the supplement as well as the complement of its predecessor.

ARRANGEMENT OF THE MODELS.

In the *arrangement of the models* the following points have been kept in view:

1. The series must progress without break from the easy to the difficult, from the simple to the complex.
2. There must be a refreshing variety both in the exercises and in the models.
3. The first models of the series should be of such a nature that they can be quickly executed. The tasks must be such that results will speedily follow, so that the children by degrees will gain sufficient confidence to undertake work requiring more extended time.
4. In making the first models, only a small number of tools should be used.
5. The models must follow in a progressive order, so that by means of the preceding work the pupils will have attained the necessary aptitude to make the succeeding without any direct help from the teacher, and consequently it will not be more difficult to make one model than another. The mak-

ing of the forty-nine previous models should render No. 50 no more difficult than No. 1 was at the outset.

6. The models must be of such a nature that the child is able to make an exact copy and not only an approximate one.

7. The knife should be used as the fundamental tool. As nearly every child knows how to use the knife, we have hereby a means of enabling the pupil to proceed from the known to the unknown.

8. Rather hard wood should be used for the first models, as it is more difficult to work with the knife upon soft wood.

TOOLS.

It is desirable that each pupil have a set of tools, and be held responsible to keep them sharp and in good order. A special cupboard should be placed in the room, wherein most of the tools can be put away after the school hours. Each tool should be numbered according to the bench to which it belongs. The art of sharpening tools must be taught.

An opinion has prevailed that the tools used in the school should be of smaller size than those of the trades. This idea was carried out in Denmark as well as in France until within recent years.

Experience shows, however, that children of the age of eleven to fourteen years are quite capable of using full-sized tools, and even manage to work better in consequence thereof, since the weight of the tool frequently assists in the doing of the work, as, for instance, in planing.

Furthermore, if small tools are used, the parents and the children are not apt to regard the work as real. We have not as yet seen any advantage attending the adoption of small tools in the manual work.

AGE OF PUPILS, LENGTH OF LESSONS, ETC.

The Nääs System is not suitable for children under ten years of age. In Sweden the Sloyd is taught in the public school to boys of the age of eleven to fourteen years. The amount of time that is devoted to it is from four to six hours a week, or, on an average, about one hundred and twenty-five hours a year.

It has been found best to extend the duration of each lesson to two hours, as one hour is too short to admit of arranging the benches, tools, and wood, as well as of doing the work, while three hours proves too great a tax upon the child's strength.

Manual work is perhaps best taught in the middle of the morning, as it then serves to break the monotony of too many book studies, and yet the children are not too tired to enjoy and take an interest in the exercise.

WHO SHALL BE THE TEACHER?

The teacher is the most important factor in education. As is the teacher, so are the pupils. The earnest spirit of the teacher working amid poor surroundings will bring about better results than fine premises, external advantages, and expensive apparatus. The teacher must assume a great responsibility, and for this reason artisans who are not *teachers* should not be employed to give instruction in manual wood-work.

The greatest recommendation for the artisan is his superior technical skill. The principle that must not be lost sight of is that this instruction is an educational means, and that only a teacher can properly impart his knowledge and impress it upon the child's mind. An artisan may be a good teacher, in which case he is equally qualified to instruct, and a teacher may in reality not be a teacher at all; but, as a rule, the artisan lacks a professional training—an important requisite for the making of a good teacher.

It is necessary for the teacher to take a course in manual work, and to become sufficiently acquainted with the manipulation of tools to be able not only to understand the method, but also to make the models.

SHOULD THE INSTRUCTION BE INDIVIDUAL OR CLASS TEACHING?

Manual training loses much of its educational value when it is not taught individually. Educators have agreed that the nature of the child is the basis upon which educational systems must be built. Since children have different capabilities, and since there are as many individualities as there are children, it is evident that the same instruction will not suit all.

To be sure, book studies are taught by class teaching, but this is only a sad necessity. Teachers generally are of the opinion that these subjects could be better taught individually. From an economical point of view, the only advantage in class teaching is that it permits the teacher to take more pupils under his care at one time than individual teaching does.

In the Sloyd the teacher may give instruction to a class of any number of pupils in the method of making the models, but he can neither supervise nor control the work of more than sixteen to eighteen children at one time.

In manual training, several methods of class teaching have been tried; for instance, in France and in some Danish schools the scholars have kept time while at work, going through the exercises at the command of the teacher. The result of this was that the pupils did not keep together in the amount of work accomplished, as one child with several movements of the same tool did as much work as it took another child many movements to accomplish.

Supplementary work was also attempted. This proved unsuccessful, because the boys who received the supplementary work and a repetition of the exercises were very frequently just those who needed it least; and thus, having been kept back, they were prevented from learning certain necessary manipulations, and left school without having completed the entire work. It was also found that the boy who did supplementary work required as much supervision as though he proceeded with the ordinary series.

The most common method in the class-teaching system of manual work is to allow those pupils who have finished the model to wait for the rest to catch up, without doing anything at all. The *excellence* of this method requires no comment.

Of course there are other opinions on this subject. One of our American authorities believes that class instruction is preferable, and states that individual instruction drives pupils into enforced idleness while waiting for the teacher.

In Sweden, where individual instruction has been practically applied for many years, this has only been found to be the case at the very outset. Each pupil soon became sufficiently informed to go on with the work quite independently of the teacher, since the models are arranged according to the child's capabilities. Later on, when the work became more intricate with a second model in hand, the boys have rarely, if ever, been found idle.

The London "Journal of Education," in discussing this question, says: "If the class be taught as a unit, what of the enforced idleness of those who work too fast, or of the enforced scampering of those who work too slow?"

Our American author in a former work, speaking of the Swedish Sloyd system, mentions the following three objections to this system:

1. The manual training is limited to wood-work.
2. The pupils are taught and shown about their work separately; class instruction is not given, and the several pupils in the laboratory are doing very different things.
3. The things wrought are household furniture or implements and utensils to be carried home and used there. There appears to be no aim beyond making thrifty householders.

Regarding the first objection, the advocates of the Sloyd movement regret that the author has quoted this information without due authority, for in the public schools of Stockholm, Gothenburg, and in almost all of the towns of Sweden, Sloyd metal work and Sloyd cardboard work have been taught for many years.

The second objection—namely, to individual instruction—is not treated at all in this earlier book, and in the later one is confined entirely to the "enforced idleness while waiting for the teacher" theory. The author likewise promises to show that "the evils resulting from class instruction" are not real, but only apparent evils. This still remains to be shown.

In regard to the third objection, in which it is claimed that the objects should be of less importance than the method and aim of the work, the question arises whether the making of "thrifty householders" should not be an aim in public education.

The same author continues: "The attractiveness of the Swedish word *Slöyd* is that (to us) it has no etymological meaning to bias us. It shall forever mean to us just what we see it means when we see the things that the Swedes call by that name."

In spite of this statement, it seems that the Sloyd has a special meaning for this author, which, though not an etymological one, nevertheless biases his opinion most strongly, and which he takes special care to emphasize by calling the Sloyd models "things."

Again, on close examination, these "things" will be found to contain more exercises in woodworking than any series of wood models used in our American manual training schools, which are, practically speaking, high schools, and for which the Sloyd system is not intended.

The slight put by so great and eminent a writer upon the Sloyd system is likewise imposed upon the various other European systems of educational manual training, as they are all practically ignored. This seems very strange indeed, as the European systems existed prior to the establishment of any manual training school in America, and it would be vain to deny that many of our best ideas on this subject have been gathered from the tried experiences in European institutions.

CHAPTER III.

THE HISTORY OF MANUAL TRAINING.

DEVELOPMENT OF THE MANUAL TRAINING IDEA IN VARIOUS EUROPEAN COUNTRIES.

(A Translation from the Swedish of Salamon's "Sloydskola and Folkskola," Book V.)

THE application of manual training to public education is not a new idea. The history of pedagogy for centuries back confirms this statement.

Luther and *Zwingli*, reformers of the Church and the school, have written widely on this subject.

Amos Commenius, savant and teacher, who, driven from his native town by the religious persecutions of the thirty years' war, found a home in every place where science and scientists were honored, and who, without doubt, may be called the "father of pedagogy," has in his several works shown the true significance of manual training as a means of education.

Francke, who founded the "religious direction" in pedagogy, gave instruction in wood-turning, pasteboard work, and glass-cutting at his remarkable Halle schools. Their institution dates back to the end of the sixteenth century.

John Locke, the sharp-sighted English philosopher, says in his well-known essay, "Some Thoughts Concerning Education," that children from an early age should be trained in corporal work; and he recommends carpentry and gardening.

Jean Jacques Rousseau, the many-sided genius, whose "Émile," or "On Education," is a pedagogical gold-mine (and this metaphor holds good especially when we consider that the noble metal must always be freed of much dross), requires that his pupils be taught a trade, and after careful investigation arrives at the conclusion, that of all trades carpentry is best adapted for educational purposes. "He must work like a peasant, and think like a philosopher, in order not to become good for nothing or a savage; and the great secret of education is to combine mental and physical work so that the one kind of exercise refreshes for the other."

The philanthropists *Basedow*, *Salzmann*, and *Campe* replanted Rousseau's ideas on German soil, and in their writings have laid great stress upon the manner in which they applied these principles.

Pestalozzi, who introduced intuition in instruction, and love in education, speaks of the importance of a methodical arrangement in the teaching of manual training.

Herbart, the creator of the newer scientific pedagogics, sees in hand-labor an almost indispensable means of building up the child's character, and especially the power of self-reliance.

Friedrich Froebel, founder of the "Kindergarten," thinks that activity exists before knowledge, and is the cause of it. He places manual work in the center of the instruction system, and groups all the other studies around it.

It is not only these great thinkers who have recognized the importance of manual instruction. Many suggestions, both theoretical and practical, have come from other sources, and more especially so during the last twenty years, since the question of manual training and its place among school subjects has become one of the day.

The following are the names of some of the educators who have been much interested in this work, and whose ideas are worthy of our careful consideration.

Martin Planta (1727–1772), a Swiss clergyman of evangelical faith, who in many respects may be regarded as the predecessor of his great countryman Pestalozzi, introduced at the Haldenstein school near Chur, which was afterward moved to the Castle of Marschlin, a system of manual work for educational purposes. He busied his pupils with wood-turning, pasteboard work, glass-cutting, gardening, and similar occupations. Barometers, thermometers, and various physical and mathematical instruments were made. Planta's activity was limited entirely to this institution.

Ferdinand Kinderman (1740–1801), the Bohemian school reformer, at this time advanced the idea of introducing manual work in the public elementary schools. It is to him that is due the honor of being the first to bring this question into public discussion. In his work " Von der Entstehung und Verbreitungs-art der Industrie Klassen in der Volkschulen des Königsreichs Böhmens " (" An Account of the Origin and Increase of the Industrial Classes in the Public Schools of the Kingdom of Bohemia "), Kinderman says : " After carefully examining the work of our primary schools, it became apparent to me that the children were least of all occupied with those studies which would be of most service to them after the school period. I became convinced that this was the cause of much laziness and poverty, of unfruitful religious life, of neglect of God's decrees, and of great wickedness. I set myself the task of studying the nature of the child. The common opinion that much can be done with the young mind contributed largely to strengthen me in my determination to carry out my ideas.

"Before long I became convinced that our primary schools, even if they are worthy of being followed as examples in some respects, certainly do not come up to the highest standards, and, besides, do not in any way fulfill the aim of preparing the pupils for their life-work. It is not enough to cram the heads full of information, and take no step to create a love for work. Working classes and reading classes must be combined. This is the only way that industry can be made a national characteristic. I became all the more eager to bring about a reform, as my experience taught me that the most industrious people were always the most moral."

Kinderman established a school in Kaplitz, a small town in Budweiser Kreitz, where he likewise officiated as clergyman. In 1773 this school became a state normal college, and was enlarged in accordance with Kinderman's ideas. His work was appreciated so much, that in 1781, according to his account, some two hundred manual training departments were organized in connection with the primary schools of Bohemia. Instruction was given to boys and girls in spinning and knitting, and in some classes manual wood-working was taught.

Von Helfest, the author of the "Austrian Primary School," says in this work: "We have little left of Kinderman's great labor, except the healthy effect that can still be traced as a direct result of his work. If Bohemia's industries rank highest in Austria, among the causes that have brought about this happy result the influence of the great schoolman, Ferdinand Kinderman, will not be forgotten. He had hardly any public support, but by his great wisdom and untiring energy he urged a collaboration with men of all classes. He has made the primary school the foundation of the welfare of our state. If you will ask the majority of those who during the early part of the century were successful farmers, thriving merchants, or wealthy manufacturers, to what cause they would attribute the first source of their material prosperity, I am sure they will without exception answer: 'It was the school which gave us the love and desire for work, and showed us the blessing of industry, order, and economy.'"

In evangelical Germany, the first manual training school was established in Göttingen in 1784, by *L. G. Wageman*, a clergyman, who was deeply attached to the cause of increasing the general usefulness of mankind. Following the example of the work of this institution, many others of a similar nature were founded at the end of the last and the beginning of the present century.

Heppe, in his "Geschichte des Deutschen Volkschulwesens" ("History of the Condition of the German Public Schools"), talks much about their organization and growth. He states that such schools were established in Lippe-Detmold, 1788; Wurzburg, 1789; Hanover, 1790; Braunschweig, 1792; Wurtemburg, 1795; Prussia, 1798; Gotha, 1798; Baden, 1803; Bavaria, 1804; Hesse, 1808. These "Industrieschulen" (Industrial Schools) were intended exclusively for the poorer classes, and their aim was to instil the love for work as a human duty.

Arnold Wageman, a brother of the clergyman of Göttingen, published in 1791 a book entitled "Über die Bildung des Volks zur Industrie" ("On the Education of the Masses for Industrial Pursuits"), wherein the word "industrie" is defined as "an employment of time and energy to the best ends, conforming to the laws of economy." He speaks of the aim of the industrial schools, as follows:

"We cannot expect any good influence from the home training, unless in the home can be found persons who perfectly understand the relation of education to 'industrie.' Therefore this work must at present be carried on in the schools. It is there that from an early age the child should be trained in such occupations as will exercise and develop those forces which can and will later on be usefully applied. Up to the present time we have not done so. We have occupied the child's mind with subjects which are of no real importance to him, and upon which his attention has remained only as long as there were external means at work, such as either his love for the teacher or his fear of punishment. How can such compulsory activity be useful to the mind?

"I am bold enough to say that it is wrong to begin school work with direct instruction in subjects that are purely mental, and amount to nothing more than memory lessons, since the child has had no experience, and it is only experience that can give interest to the study of abstract subjects. It would certainly be better to follow the hints offered by Nature, who allows the growth of the body in early childhood to supersede that of the mind. We should, therefore, put a greater demand upon the more rapidly growing corporal forces than upon the brain with its slower development.

"The youthful strength has been stunted rather than invigorated. What child can understand the necessity of all this uncomfortable sitting still and all these memory lessons? The child must have an aim in his work, an aim very near to his heart, if we wish him to achieve the desired result. How often does it happen that the real pleasure the child experiences when leaving the school exists in aught else than the consciousness of being finally able to give vent to forces that have been held in check?

"We need only, unobserved by the children, watch them at their occupations after school hours. We will soon see how we ought to busy them in the class-room, in order to make their school life both agreeable and useful.

"The boys will be found at the brooks, building dams and water-wheels, making grottos, constructing cottages, or possibly carrying wood and other material on little wagons. Some choose more difficult, others more easy tasks, depending upon their natural boldness.

"The girls play with dolls, though these may be made of nothing but leaves and moss, and they often imitate housekeeping in their games.

"All want activity, and thus they compensate themselves for the sitting still in the schoolroom. Can these facts not teach us how we ought to occupy our little ones? Rapidly they go from one pastime to another; perseverance is not their forte, and still we are to make steady workmen out of them. Do we employ the right means, when we keep them for six hours a day at their desks?"

Wageman gives us a concise rule as a guide in teaching manual work. He says: "As a most elementary principle, we must follow Nature's way, and choose at the beginning such work as shall require both little mental and physical labor, so that the results may be quickly attained. The instruction must be thorough, and the attention must be closely riveted, and only at the outset should poor or faulty work be tolerated."

Dr. I. G. Krünitz, a contemporary of Wageman, has treated this subject more at length in his work "Die Landschulen so wohl wie Lehr als auch Arbeits oder Industrie Schulen Betrachtet"

("The Country Schools Viewed as Instruction and Manual or Industrial Schools"). This work was published in 1794, and by a royal mandate was ordered to be bought by every parish in Prussia.

He says: "The time devoted to book studies might be much decreased if theoretical and practical work were combined; and, since we have arrived at the conclusion that more will be learned in this way, one might say that the half has become greater than the whole. Book work alone is very unproductive of good results, as is proven by the fact that our country boys, after spending six hours per day at school during a period of from six to eight years, are in most cases ignorant, rough, and illiterate."

This book contains many practical suggestions concerning the arrangement of manual instruction, as well as accounts of the public schools in which manual training has been introduced.

At this time a similar movement was going on in France. The great revolution against all the old customs had just begun. In the words of Mirabeau, " pour tout reconstruire été forcé de tout démolir" ("in order to reconstruct everything, everything must first be destroyed"). The signs of the early period gave promise of an entire change in the form of public instruction, and a well-arranged plan embodying the new ideas on manual work was adopted.

In a comprehensive and interesting book entitled "L'instruction Public en France Pendant la Revolution," published in Paris in 1881, *Hippeau* says: "All principles of education and all systems of instruction have been studied and developed from the point of view of a government which through the grace of God has been founded from the ruins of a kingdom, by the national will. Our education should have, as its starting point, a respect for the rights of man, and should be arranged to suit the needs and demands of a people who but a short time ago acquired their liberty."

The National Assembly now exhibited a peculiar drama. At the same time that it crushed out all that seemed to stand as an obstacle in the way of the new order of things, executing thereby the most terrible and bloodthirsty acts, it interested itself in the study of all matters pertaining to the education of the masses, with a calmness and judgment most astonishing in its strong contrast to the perpetration of its dreadful deeds.

In 1793, the year that witnessed the falling of

the heads of the king and queen before the guillotine, when terrorism raged at its highest, the convention worked with great eagerness to establish throughout the excited republic new schools embodying the new ideas. At no time before or since have these questions played so prominent a part in public debate, and caused so much general discussion, as during these eventful times.

Hippeau further says: "To the time of the convention can be traced the origin of the idea of introducing manual work in the elementary schools."

On the 13th of July, 1793, *Robespierre* laid before the National Assembly a plan of education which was to be followed throughout the republic. This plan had been drawn up by *Michael le Peletier*, a member of the Assembly, who was murdered in January of the same year. Robespierre was its warmest advocate.

The following is an extract from this plan: "Public education, besides giving strength and health, must instil the duty of the habit of work, because this is to all both a necessity and an advantage. I do not refer to a thorough knowledge of any particular kind of work, but rather to that energy, that activity, that industriousness, and that perseverance to the end, which characterize the life of every diligent individual. Educate such men, and the republic will see its fruits of agriculture and of industry redoubled. Instil in the child this need, this habit of work, and his future existence is secured, as he will then be entirely dependent upon himself. I consider this part of education as the most important, and therefore my plan of general instruction contains manual labor as its vital feature. Of all the sources which are apt to stimulate the average child, none will produce a greater desire for activity than physical work.

" By this bill which I lay before you, I hope to interest fathers, teachers, and pupils. Fathers, because their taxes will be decreased; teachers, because they may hope for honor and recompense in this new field; and children, because the accomplishment of some real, material work will always be to them a source of great delight. I would desire that various kinds of handicraft work might be introduced."

In spite of Robespierre's efforts, this question remained for almost a century at a stand-still, and it was not until the era of the third republic that the ideas of the first were carried into execution. Let us return for a moment to the progress in Germany.

A. H. Niemeyer (1754–1828), rector of the University of Halle, and director of the institutions founded by Francke, in his well-known work, " Die Grundsätze der Erziehung und des Unterrichtes " (" The Principles of Education and Instruction "), says : " The more incessantly we employ the children, the more we can shield them from evil habits, and create in them a desire for the good. Children for whom otherwise there seemed no hope, needed but very little correction as soon as a means for keeping them actively employed was found. To discover an occupation suitable to each stage of development, is without doubt the important work of every educational system. We should therefore give the children an opportunity to become mentally and physically active, and should not tax them beyond their natural forces. Manual work strengthens the body, and frees the home life from dullness and *ennui*.

" Of the many kinds of physical labor, the *carpentry* may be considered as the most suitable handicraft for the young, on account of the many works that can be accomplished in it, and also on account of the great variety of tools employed.

Carpentry is not beyond the natural powers of the child. Turnery exercises the senses and creates an artistic faculty. It is well to teach the child how to handle such tools as are used in the home, as the saw, the hammer, the ax, the auger, etc. Neglecting this, we are really making our children helpless, since they will be unable to use the common tools without hurting themselves."

In 1797 a pamphlet appeared entitled, "Über die Benützung des bei Kindern so thätigen Triebes, beschäftigt zu sein" ("How to Make Use of the Child's Active Impulse to be Occupied"). The author, *J. H. G. Heusinger* (1766-1837), doctor of philosophy and pedagogy at the University of Jena, is, generally speaking, to be regarded as the predecessor of Froebel, as he begins with very nearly the same principles, and arrives at similar conclusions.

Rissmann says: "Heusinger's works were very carefully studied by Froebel. His books owned by Froebel were all marked with many marginal notes. It is needless to say that this does not in any way detract from the practical value of Froebel's pedagogy." Much stress is laid upon the development of the sense of beauty, for which reason Heusinger believes that modeling should form a part of the school work.

The following is a short extract from his remarkable writings : " From the sixth year on, the children are taught from books. Is it at all surprising that they think it is from books alone that knowledge is to be obtained? A bright child has therefore no other desire than to get books and to study out of them. The acquisition of knowledge by his own observation, by his own efforts, is something that our present education does not teach him. This is left for after school hours, because it is still believed that the teaching of facts should be the main feature of all educational systems."

Heusinger shows us in his book " Die Familie Wertheim " (" The Family Wertheim "), how his principles are best to be applied. He shows that the instruction must be founded upon experiences gathered by those who are closely watching the school work. He thinks that manual work should be a principal means of education, as it satisfies the child's natural desire for creating and imitating.

Regarding the choice of occupation, he believes —first, that the occupation should correspond with the physical forces; secondly, that the work should not impair the child's health; thirdly, that it should be executed both while sitting and standing, thus giving opportunity to frequently change the position of the body; fourthly, that the work should not only be the means of making the future apprenticeship to the trades easier, but should be of general use in any vocation; fifthly, that materials should be chosen from which many different objects can be made; sixthly, that the main stress should be laid upon the connection between the practical work and the acquisition of true knowledge; and, finally, that the work should develop the sense of form and beauty. To accomplish all this, Heusinger proposes pasteboard, bone, wax, metal, and wood work.

Emanuel von Fellenberg (1771–1844), founder of Hofwyl, as he liked to call himself, partly collaborating with Pestalozzi, strove to develop a national system of education. Hofwyl was an estate situated several miles north of Bern, Switzerland. Fellenberg bought this in 1799, and turned it into a colony which to-day might serve as a model for agricultural and industrial work. Among all the institutions founded there, the well-known " Poor School " was his favorite. The motto of the school was " Pray and Work," and he told his pupils again and again that truly industrious men not only produce more than dull, mechanical workers, but are really able to do the state a greater and higher service.

In this school the pupils were principally occupied in the fields, in the woods, in housework, and in the shops. As a recreation, instruction was given in theoretical studies. One who witnessed what was done here says: "The instruction given was indeed refreshing. The boys would come from an arduous task, and would return to it with renewed energy and readiness. I can only explain this on the ground that they were spurred on by the existence of an inner mental joy."

Here are Fellenberg's words: "Philanthropists, come and rejoice with me in the blessed experience of the fact that the necessity of earning one's own bread can be productive of better results than the dwarfing of mental and corporal forces, and that physical exertion under correct guidance may be of great and lasting benefit to both mind and body." In his school for boys of the higher classes, in which, during a period of some ten years, the sons of the most renowned families of Europe, and even princes of the reigning houses, were pupils, manual instruction was given in wood and pasteboard work.

Johann Jacob Wehrli (1790–1855) was for many years the director of the poor school at Hofwyl.

Though a plain and simple man, who never had the advantage of a higher education, he nevertheless possessed just those qualities which eminently fitted him to be a teacher of the poor. He followed Pestalozzi's method of instruction, placing all matters before the children in the most intelligible and practical light.

The education for work being the chief aim of the school, little time was devoted to the usual studies. Wehrli gave much chance instruction. When at work, he told many instructive tales, and sometimes he would even require the children to solve problems in arithmetic; and at the same time, in the most natural way, he would tell them facts connected with the practical work which they had in hand.

Through his efforts, the scholars learned to work in a thoughtful manner. He loved his pupils as a father, and nursed them as a mother. In later years, many schools with his method were founded throughout Germany, and such have been called "Wehrli schools."

Bernhard Heinrich Blasche was to Salzmann what Wehrli was to Fellenberg; namely, a highly esteemed contemporary. Blasche superintended the so-called "mechanical work." A man of much experience as a teacher, he has expressed the value of manual labor as an educational influence in his numerous writings, the best known of which, " Die Werstätte der Kinder," is an extensive and interesting work in four volumes. His views, like Rousseau's, are that manual training should be taught as a basis for intellectual improvement.

J. G. Fichte (1762–1814), in his well-known speeches to the German nation, points out the importance of incorporating manual training into the national educational system, and says that it is the only means for the fatherland's regeneration. " My chief request is that theoretical instruction and practical labor be combined, so that each school will appear self-supporting to its scholars, thereby creating a desire in each pupil to contribute his share of work in accordance with his capabilities.

" Without touching upon the feasibility or the economical practicability of such a method of instruction—questions which rightfully belong to our proposition—my request arises as a direct result of the aim of true education, partly because the majority of those who are instructed under the national educational system belong to the workingmen's classes, whose early training should without doubt be in the line of technical work, and more especially because there will arise in the young a consciousness of being able to shift for themselves, and a reluctance to rely upon the munificence of others.

"This is surely the sole condition of each man's self-respect. If we were to investigate the careers of those who have led a bad or demoralized life, we should always find that they would neither learn to work, nor to understand the true habit of economy.

"Our idea is to teach the young how to work, so that in the future they will not be tempted to commit crime in order to satisfy the mere needs of existence. We would in no case except those who intend to follow a learned career from this kind of work."

Schindler, a prominent Swiss statesman, in 1854 gave to the public the following prize question: "How shall the instruction in our elementary schools be freed from its present abstract method, and be made more conducive to true mental development?" This question was the cause of many competitive writings, among which may be mentioned essays from the most prominent pedagogues of the day.

The newspapers discussed the matter, and held it in its true light before the eyes of the public.

The pedagogical value of manual education was at once suggested.

Among the valuable answers, two deserve special mention; viz., " Die Arbeits-schulen der Land-gemeinden in ihren voll-berechtigten zusammenwirken mit der Lehrschulen " (" The Working Schools of the Parishes in their True Relation to the Elementary Schools") by **Dr. Conrad Michelson**, and " Die Erziehung zur Arbeit, eine Forderung des Lebens an die Schule " (" The Education to Work, a Demand which Life makes of the School ") by Karl Friedrich. We give a few extracts from these works.

Proceeding from Fichte's statement that the public education was the important problem of the period, Michelson tried to prove that the solution could be more easily reached by connecting the elementary schools, which at that time were simply reading schools, with the so-called working schools. The author speaks of those founded in 1796, by *Duke Peter of Oldenburg*, in Holstein. This warm-hearted nobleman, feeling that he had not done sufficient by simply granting freedom to his serfs, and knowing " that he who is free must understand how to use his liberty, how to busy the mind, and employ the hands," established manual schools in which spinning, sewing, and weaving were taught to girls, wood-work to boys, and gardening to both.

Dr. Conrad Michelson, who had made a close study of these schools, says: " I spent much time talking to men and women who had been educated there; I found that though many had forgotten the most of that which had been taught in the reading schools, the working school was still living in their grateful recollections, and they all, without exception, acknowledged the valuable habits they had acquired there."

In another chapter he says: " When it is necessary to fight against a deeply rooted disease, the facts of the case must be taken as they are, and not as one would like them to be. I could tell you many curious facts about these families.

"I recall one instance of a father who had been an habitual drunkard, and who worked only when urgent necessity drove him to it. His son had joined one of these working schools, and busied himself evenings by doing some little manual work. One evening the father became interested in the son's work, and it was not a long time after this that he was encouraged to take a hand in it. He has since become thrifty and useful. I know of another case, where, through the influence of a daughter, the good taught in the school was reflected as a blessing in the house.

"To you who believe only in figures, I can show by figures that a large part of the expenses which working schools will entail would in reality be saved out of the funds which are now expended on the poor-house."

According to Michelson, all articles of luxury should be excluded from the manual work, for the same reason that all abstract subjects should be omitted from the book studies. His motto is, "Erziehen, nicht Verziehen" ("Guidance, not Misguidance"). It is not *models* we want, but the habit to work. Referring to the models, he says: "On this rock many a manual training school has been wrecked." The kind of work must be arranged in accordance with the sphere in which the pupils live, so that they may in a measure become prepared for their future occupations. The country boys should be instructed in Klütern* (manual training in wood-work) and in plaiting.

---

* The expression *Klütern*, taken from the Holstein dialect, corresponds to the Swedish *Träsloyd* (wood-sloyd). According to Michelson, *Klütern* signifies all kinds of wood-work, both for home and field industry, such work as does not apply to any particular trade. Duke Peter's statement, that the aim of the country working school should be to produce various objects in wood for the home, the stable, the barn, and the field, expressed the same idea.

Karl Friedrich's " Erziehung zur Arbeit" ("Education to Work"), written with much care and in a clear, persuasive tone, is a work of great merit which exerted a wide influence. It has attracted considerable attention, and is still used as a book of reference. Those who in the main sympathize with this author will find him at times dealing in exaggerations, and again wandering in idealistic dreamland

In the first four chapters, to which is prefixed the "Können ist besser denn Wissen" ("To be Able is better than to Know"), Friedrich explains what seem to him to be the faults that underlie the elementary school system. He says: "Some of the subjects are not proportionately valuable to the amount of time devoted to them; what is learned is very soon forgotten." The following quotations furnish a good illustration of Karl Friedrich's opinions:

"In 1882 a committee on instruction in Belgium examined 8,917 young soldiers. Of this number, 7,861 had attended either a public or a private elementary school. The following results were obtained: Of 2,347 young men who could not write, 1,877 had taken a primary school education. Of 6,480 who could write, 1,476 could not add the figures 492, 102, 18; 3,120 did not know how many meters there are in one kilometer; 684 did not know in which country London is situated; and 4,047 did not know whether Moses lived before or after Christ.

"Purely mental exertion impedes healthy bodily development. In a certain community in Saxony, out of 1,604 young men who were to be enrolled in the military service, 902 were found physically incapable, 176 partially incapable, and 199 beneath the required stature. In a certain part of Prussia, among 17,246 young men, who on account of having passed special examinations were only to serve for one year in the army, 80% were found physically incapable.

"In the work of the public school, a great disproportion exists between the teaching force and the number of pupils, and therefore it becomes impossible for the most zealous teacher to occupy all the children under his care, and to keep proper discipline. He is sure to be overworked and physically enfeebled.

"The continuous still sitting, and the teaching of subjects which neither attract nor hold the child's attention, are the reasons why no real desire for knowledge is engendered; and when the children work with eagerness and apparent pleasure, it is generally due to other means than an interest in the subject itself. The present instruction neither corresponds with what the true aim of the public school should be, nor with the laws that directly relate to the nature of the child.

"The cause of these sad truths may be found in the fact that the school has been changed from an institution which should be a means to an end, into one that has concentrated its entire aim within itself. Instead of at every stage adapting its instruction to the requirements of the after-school period, it dogmatically follows out its own ideas regarding the subjects to be taught, and the degree of perfection to which each study is to be carried. What is the result? We force our children to abide by a system which is opposed to their natural desires, since they prefer the golden fruits of life to grave and ponderous theories.

"By making the instruction more practical than it has hitherto been, we can best effect a true preparation. So long as the school teaches only theoretical subjects, it will continue to become more and more proud of these, and will instil an air of superiority toward the home and the life outside of the school. A purely practical element would furnish reactionary means.

This tendency to do practical and physical work is a demand of human nature, especially visible in the young, since they not only require a harmonious development, but also can have their desire for activity best satisfied in this way.

"The advantage of a practical discipline can be explained by stating that the method must proceed from the simplest and most convenient to the more difficult and involved exercises of the powers; thus being opposed to the theoretical method, which usually proceeds from complicated abstractions, which of necessity strain and confuse the pupils.

"Since practical work is consistent with the nature of the youth, there is no particular need of awakening an interest by artificial or compulsory means. Pedagogy itself will accomplish through practical instruction that which it conceives as its first duty; namely, it will secure by investigation a correct knowledge of the true characteristics of its pupils.

"Individuality presupposes a distinct self-activity, and can never be the result of receptivity alone. Every teacher has known boys who were remarkable for their dullness while at school, and who, when put in other surroundings, became active and useful, while some of the so-called excellent pupils grew to be lazy and unprincipled men.

"When we think of the sickness and deformity caused by the leaning positions assumed by both teacher and pupils, it requires no argument to convince us of the advantages to health and physical development to be gained from the practical work.

"The greatest advantage of manual work is its influence on the character and moral nature, which renders it as much a feature of education as of instruction. Competition in this work takes a more natural and less dangerous turn, for the reason that an ambition which seeks to *do* a work more correctly is surely more natural and less dangerous than one which aims at simply *being considered* to have done something better.

"The fact that the practical instruction has a direct bearing upon the home and the family life is of a great pedagogical value, because less educated parents are able to take an interest in the progress of their children, as this work comes more within the capacity of their judgment."

Having spoken about the previous attempts made, and having explained some of the reasons why such attempts proved unsuccessful, the author tries to show a possibility of the realization of his ideas.

His book ends thus: "Whatever be the destiny of these contemplations, whether they are going to have some direct result or not, the author thinks that he has paid a debt to his fatherland, and to the youth growing up to manhood, by openly declaring what to him seems to be the real defect in the present educational system. He does not claim any originality for his proposition, but it has the advantage of being the *expression* of a thought, which perhaps for a long time has been in the minds of many fathers and many teachers."

"Die Erziehung zur Arbeit" came out in 1852. Thirty-one years later it appeared in another edition, completely revised by the author. Instead of the *nom de plume Karl Friedrich*, we find on the title-page the name of *Prof. Karl Biederman*, a prominent writer on political science. Professor Biederman took an active part in the political strife of 1848. In this second edition, the Swedish Sloyd is mentioned in a most flattering way.

In the middle of this century, while throughout Germany a great deal of activity was manifested in pedagogical circles—a period marked by numerous writings on the manual training question—*Torsten Rudenschöld* (1798–1859), the self-made schoolman as he has been called, worked with unremitting zeal to reform the Swedish public school system.

It is not so much because of what he said or wrote, but rather for what he did, and for the example he furnished to others, that many of those who have worked in the cause of education will remember him with a feeling of love and esteem, as a man whose warm heart told him what the people needed, and whose gifts as a true educator enabled him to scatter the seeds for future harvests.

To the advocates of the Swedish Sloyd instruction system, it will be pleasant to recollect that Rudenschöld did not overlook the importance of educational manual training.

In a little pamphlet which appeared in 1856 entitled, "The Practical Arrangement of the Swedish Public School," he says: "It is becoming more and more universally acknowledged, that in the elementary school the children are overburdened with continual reading lessons, which they have not had sufficient time to digest, and the result of which is a valueless memory knowledge. That the mind and the body are to be developed at the same time, is gradually coming to be more and more understood. Gymnastics is too much of a health remedy to awaken either a sufficient pleasure or interest for its own sake.

"To devote too much time to corporal work cannot be advantageous, as we do not propose to make either mechanics or physical workers of all our children; yet no one can tell the future of his child. In real life, everything rests upon an uncertain and ever changing basis. In the mercantile world, 'all is not gold that glitters.'

"The system of credits, when closely examined into, may be likened to a tremendous sphere resting upon a volcano. The pupils who are fond of speculation are walking upon it. The eruption suddenly comes. It then happens that the young men of the better classes are left without a means of self-support.

"Children of the best families, no matter how high their social position may be, will receive much benefit from an early training in physical work, as we constantly hear the complaint that they are too weak, and seek only the pleasures of life and its expensive diversions. They will then learn for themselves that in corporal work there is more true satisfaction, and will prefer it as a refreshing pastime.

"It is said of John Adams, President of the United States of America, that after spending his mornings in executive duties he would devote his leisure afternoons to farming and gardening."

In studying the history of pedagogy, in order to learn the ideas expressed by the more prominent writers on the manual training question, two names which must not be overlooked are those of Tuiskon Ziller and Uno Cygnaeus.

Tuiskon Ziller in 1864 published his scientific work entitled "Grundlegung zur Lehre von Erziehenden Unterricht" ("The Principles for the Study of Educational Instruction"). Ziller was professor of pedagogy at the University of Leipzig, and was a follower of Herbart in the true sense of the word. He discusses manual training very thoroughly.

"Its object," he says, "is to make any life's calling easier, and it should not be put in the direct service of the state by the teaching either of special trades or of manual work in the home. If the work is to be arranged so that a profit will accrue from the sale of the objects made, the future of each child will be sacrificed. This question is not to be regarded from an economical standpoint. The selling of the work would imply a continual repetition of about the same exercise, which means a thoughtless, mechanical occupation.

"The elements of various handicrafts may be taught, such as turnery, the use of the hammer, saw, plane, bore, and file. Such models must be taken from the series in which the simplest exercises are to be found, so as to avoid difficult and intricate combinations. Theoretical and practical work should as far as possible bear one another out.

"On the one hand, natural science, mathematics, grammar, history, geography, drawing, and singing should offer problems to the work-shop; and, on the other hand, the practical experiences gathered in the manual work should make book studies the more easily learned."

Ziller argues very strongly against the theory which had been previously advanced; namely, that "manual work should form the basis for all instruction whose aim is a general educational one."

Uno Cygnaeus has not come to occupy his prominent place among the educators of his time through his numerous scientific contributions to pedagogical literature. His views have been expressed less in words than in deeds. They stand forth in sharp, distinct clearness in those special school laws which put life into the public school system of Finland, and in all the principles according to which this system is now carried on. They have been subjected to the closest practical investigation, and all Finnish teachers know how well they have stood the test. Some of these principles, taken from observation of the school work, and from information given personally, are the following:

"The primary school should be organized as a general fundamental educational institution, common to the children of all classes of society. Its direction must be practical, and its system of instruction thoroughly educational. Since the mother is the chief educator in the home, the growing woman must be trained for her future vocation, and be made familiar with those facts that relate to the child's physical life and its education. To bring this about, nurseries and kindergartens should be connected with every public school. Religious and moral training, the teaching of orderliness and cleanliness, are more important requisites for the school to fulfill than the teaching of book studies. In order to promote the practical tendency in the school work, much stress must be laid upon drawing, singing, music, and manual work.

"The manual work is to be applied as a means of formal education; that is, to develop the eye to the sense of form, and the hand to dexterity, not for a particular trade, but for promoting symmetry in general, and creating orderliness and neatness. Carpentry work, turnery, and smith's work are excellent means to this end.

"The manual work is neither to be driven like a trade, nor to be regarded as a recreation or play. It must hold a position of equal importance with the other subjects. For these reasons, it must be taught by pedagogically educated persons, particularly so in the country schools, where the general teacher should also give instruction in this kind of work.

"The teacher himself must study the theory and its practical application. He must have a true conception of its aim as a means of formal training, and he must have learned most of the manipulations so as to be able to properly direct his class. I do not underestimate theoretical lessons; I believe that all work, even the roughest manual labor, presupposes a mental motive and a mental aim.

"Just as the masses, who form the germ of society, should receive a higher education in order to acquire a nobler, more moral, and more ideal ambition for whatever work they may have chosen, so should the so-called better class be taught that God has not given the hands merely as limbs for taking food and drink, but rather as the most useful and ingenious of tools.

"I do not forget that the hand guides the pen, the paint-brush, and the operation knife, and I also value such wonderful work as it has achieved in these directions; but I would lay stress upon general hand dexterity as a most important acquisition to each and every one. Those of high or low station who possess this valuable treasure will better understand its worth in others.

"Teach the child general manual dexterity, and the practical work will in time take a position of honor. The strife between capital and labor will then be made far less severe."

CHAPTER IV.

ALFRED JOHANNSON'S NÄÄS MODEL SERIES.

OTTO SALAMON'S INTRODUCTION.

(Translated from the Swedish.)

IN questions relating to educational matters, there is no danger so great as that of remaining at a stand-still. These questions, like all things in this universe, are continually undergoing change. Much that was yesterday found desirable can to-day hardly be used, and will to-morrow be discarded altogether.

It is easy to admit the truth of this fact, without committing one's self to the error of saying that all that is old is bad, and all that is new, good. There are truths which can never grow old, though they may at times appear disguised under new forms; while, on the other hand, many new ideas seem excellent until they have been subjected to the actual tests of experience, when they are found to be utterly impracticable.

In educational matters, the golden mean must be chosen. On the one hand, we must be careful not to stagnate, not to offer ourselves as prey to the advocates of the old methods; but, on the other hand, we should seek to avoid that restless anxiety to change a system of education which has hardly had time to be submitted to a fair trial, for a newer system which has perhaps never been tried at all.

The true teacher will adopt the method which in his opinion is best calculated to produce a full development of the faculties, and will then see that his method is carefully and systematically carried out. The teacher soon finds, by experience, that in educational matters "things are not always as they seem," and what appears clear and simple may really be of a very complex nature.

The experienced teacher is careful not to jump at conclusions concerning any method; he is not satisfied to accept what others may say regarding it, nor is he willing even to trust to his own judgment; but, before he will adopt a new method, he must know from personal observation and experience what results it yields.

Educational Sloyd, one of the latest educational methods, is as yet in its first stage of development. The fundamental principles which govern it are clearly defined, but the question as to the most advantageous application of these principles is still an open one. We have taken advantage of the investigations and suggestions made by others, and have availed ourselves of the results of their wide experiences. This applies in particular to the selection of our present series of models. A series of models which a few years ago was considered practicable is now found to be unsuitable.

In an institution such as that at Nääs, where the avowed aim is to educate teachers, any neglect to keep pace with the spirit of the times would have been inexcusable. The experiences gained from each course of instruction have been invaluable, and we have profited by the suggestions of the students themselves.

Three hours a week were devoted to discussion, and it was then that each student had an opportunity to express his ideas on the subject. In this way, with hundreds of eyes watching and criticising our work, it was comparatively easy to discover and correct the errors in the system. These changes, however, have not always been found to be improvements, and it has often been necessary to reinstate the older methods.

The Nääs method, in contradistinction to the Nääs system, is that particular method which adopts the *exercises* of carpentry Sloyd as a basis for the educational manual Sloyd. Neither tools nor models should form the basis of any method; for exercises performed with one tool do not become more or less difficult when practiced with the assistance of other tools, and models are merely chance expressions of various combinations of exercises. By exercises we mean work done by the use of tools, in accordance with definite rules, designed to meet special purposes.

The statement that "the models of the series are to be arranged in consecutive order according to their comparative difficulty, proceeding from the simple to the complex," refers, therefore, to the series of exercises to be used, more than to the models which are the embodiment of the work done in these exercises.

As to the choice of models, the following rules should be observed:

1. All articles of luxury should be excluded, and the models should have a practical value.
2. The models should be such as can be finished by the pupils themselves.

3. They should be made entirely of wood; some of soft and others of hard wood.

4. As little material as possible should be used.

5. The work should not require polish.

6. The models should require little or no turning and carving.

7. They should develop the sense of form and beauty.

8. The construction of the series of models should require the use of all necessary tools, and the performance of the most important manipulations connected with wood-work.

The practical work at the Nääs Seminarium originally consisted of but one series of models. This has been changed so that the student can work out such a series as will be best adapted to the school in which it is to be used. We have at present three series with nearly the same exercises. Wherever possible, the same models are used in each of the three series.

The three series of the Nääs system are: "The Fundamental Series for Country Elementary Schools," "The Town Elementary School Series for Boys," and the "Higher Boys' School Series." The series for higher girls' schools has not as yet been completed.

OTTO SALAMON.

Nääs, *March* 18, 1890.

THE NÄÄS MODELS.

I. Models in the Fundamental Series.

(A Series for the Country Elementary Schools.)

I. a. Kindergarten pointer.
I. b. Kindergarten pointer.
II. Rake tooth.
III. Round flower stick.
IV. Penholder.
V. Rectangular flower stick.
VI. Slate-pencil holder.
VII. Key label.
VIII. Thread winder.
IX. Dibble.
X. Harness pin.
XI. Paper-cutter.
XII. a. Pail handle.
XII. b. Part of an ox-bow.
XIII. Small bowl.
XIV. Hammer handle.
XV. Spoon.
XVI. Chopping board.
XVII. Flower-pot cross.
XVIII. Scythe sharpener.
XIX. Scoop.
XX. Clothes-rack.
XXI. Flower-pot stand.
XXII. Ax handle.
XXIII. Footstool.
XXIV. Barrel cover.
XXV. Box.
XXVI. Ladle.
XXVII. Baker's shovel.
XXVIII. Clothes-beater.
XXIX. Ruler.
XXX. Bootjack.
XXXI. Lamp bracket.
XXXII. Weaving shuttle.
XXXIII. Knife box.
XXXIV. American ax handle.
XXXV. Match box.
XXXVI. Baseball bat.
XXXVII. Meter measure.
XXXVIII. Pen box.
XXXIX. Stool.
XL. Try-square.
XLI. Plate rack.
XLII. Marking gauge.
XLIII. Rake head.
XLIV. Picture frame.
XLV. Tool rack.
XLVI. Dough trough.

THE NÄÄS MODELS

XLVII. Book-stand.
XLVIII. Hooped bucket.
XLIX. Cabinet.
L. Table.

II. Models in the Town Elementary Series.
(A Series for the City Public Schools.)

I. *a.* Kindergarten pointer.
I. *b.* Kindergarten pointer.
II. Parcel pin.
III. Round flower stick.
IV. Penholder.
V. Rectangular flower stick.
VI. Slate-pencil holder.
VII. Key label.
VIII. Thread winder.
IX. Bar.
X. Pen rest.
XI. Paper-cutter.
XII. Strop stick.
XIII. Small bowl.
XIV. Hammer handle.
XV. Spoon.
XVI. Chopping board.
XVII. Flower-pot cross.
XVIII. Meter measure.
XIX. Scoop.
XX. Clothes rack.
XXI. Flower-pot stand.
XXII. Ax handle.
XXIII. Footstool.
XXIV. Book carrier.
XXV. Box.
XXVI. Ladle.
XXVII. Baker's shovel.
XXVIII. Clothes-beater.
XXIX. Ruler.
XXX. Bootjack.
XXXI. Lamp bracket.
XXXII. Weaving shuttle.
XXXIII. Knife box.
XXXIV. American ax handle.
XXXV. Match box.
XXXVI. Baseball bat.
XXXVII. Triangle.
XXXVIII. Pen box.
XXXIX. Stool.
XL. Try-square.
XLI. Plate rack.
XLII. Marking gauge.
XLIII. Rake head.
XLIV. Picture frame.
XLV. Tool rack.
XLVI. Dough trough.
XLVII. Book stand.
XLVIII. Hooped bucket.
XLIX. Cabinet.
L. Table.

III. Models in the High-School Series.

I. a. Kindergarten pointer.
I. b. Kindergarten pointer.
II. Parcel pin.
III. Round flower stick.
IV. Letter opener.
V. Rectangular flower stick.
VI. Charcoal and pencil holder.
VII. Key label.
VIII. Pack-thread winder.
IX. Bar.
X. Pen rest.
XI. Paper-cutter.
XII. Strop stick.
XIII. Small bowl.
XIV. Hammer handle.
XV. Pen tray.
XVI. Chopping board.
XVII. Flower-pot cross.
XVIII. Meter measure.
XIX. Scoop.
XX. Clothes rack.
XXI. Flower-pot stand.
XXII. Flower-press roller and rests.
XXIII. Footstool.
XXIV. Book carrier.
XXV. Box.
XXVI. Ladle.
XXVII. Flower-press.
XXVIII. Coat stretcher.
XXIX. Ruler.
XXX. Bootjack.
XXXI. Lamp bracket.
XXXII. Weaving shuttle.
XXXIII. Knife box.
XXXIV. American ax handle.
XXXV. Match box.
XXXVI. Baseball bat.
XXXVII. Triangle.
XXXVIII. Pen box.
XXXIX. Stool.
XL. Try-square.
XLI. Drawing board with frame.
XLII. Marking gauge.
XLIII. Bracket.
XLIV. Picture frame.
XLV. Tool rack.
XLVI. Tea tray.
XLVII. Book stand.
XLVIII. Hooped bucket.
XLIX. Cabinet.
L. Table.

THE NÄÄS MODELS

Exercises in the Nääs Model Series.

I. Long cut with knife.
II. Cross cut with knife.
III. Oblique cut with knife.
IV. Bevel cut with knife.
V. Sawing off.
VI. Convex cut with knife.
VII. Long or rip sawing.
VIII. Edge planing.
IX. Squaring.
X. Gauging.
XI. Boring with brace and shell-bit.
XII. Face planing.
XIII. Filing.
XIV. Boring with brace and center-bit.
XV. Convex sawing.
XVI. Concave cut with knife.
XVII. Bevel planing.
XVIII. Modeling or shaping with plane.
XIX. Cross-cut sawing with tenon or back saw.
XX. Wave sawing.
XXI. Plane surface cut.
XXII. Scraping.
XXIII. Obstacle planing.
XXIV. Perpendicular chiseling.
XXV. Oblique chiseling.
XXVI. Gouging with gouge and spoon-iron.
XXVII. Concave chiseling.
XXVIII. Chopping.
XXIX. Smoothing with spokeshave.
XXX. Modeling or shaping with spokeshave.
XXXI. Oblique sawing.
XXXII. Oblique planing (tapering).
XXXIII. Smoothing up.
XXXIV. End planing.
XXXV. Halving with knife.
XXXVI. Working in hard wood.
XXXVII. Fitting in pegs.
XXXVIII. Beveling with oblique position.

XXXIX. Gluing.
XL. Boring with brad-awl.
XLI. Sinking iron plates.
XLII. Nailing.
XLIII. Punching in nails.
XLIV. Beveling or chamfering with draw-knife.
XLV. Perpendicular gouging.
XLVI. Plain jointing.
XLVII. Dovetail clamping (oblique grooving).
XLVIII. Oblique gouging.
XLIX. Chamfering with chisel.
L. Circular sawing.
LI. Fixing with screws.
LII. Modeling with draw-knife.
LIII. Square planing (across the grain).
LIV. Wedge planing (smoothing plane).
LV. Planing with round or compass plane.
LVI. Fixing with wooden pegs (for planing thin wood).
LVII. Straight edge grooving.
LVIII. Dovetailing (common).
LIX. Planing with use of shooting-board.
LX. Scooping out with outside gouge.
LXI. Axle fitting (applied only to shuttle).
LXII. Housing or square grooving.
LXIII. Long oblique planing.
LXIV. Setting out (marking divisions with chisel).
LXV. Grooving with knife and chisel.
LXVI. Gluing with use of clamps.
LXVII. Sawing with keyhole saw.
LXVIII. Oblique edge grooving.
LXIX. Slotting (mortising with saw and chisel).

LXX. Dovetailing in thick wood.
LXXI. Mitering.
LXXII. Mortising (common and oblique).
LXXIII. Halving with saw and chisel.
LXXIV. Rabbeting.
LXXV. Graving with V-tool.
LXXVI. Half-lap dovetailing.
LXXVII. Fixing hinges.
LXXVIII. Fixing lock.
LXXIX. Double oblique dovetailing.
LXXX. Oblique notching.
LXXXI. Half-concealed edge-grooving.
LXXXII. Hollowing with plane.
LXXXIII. Fixing bottom of bucket.
LXXXIV. Hooping.
LXXXV. Haunched tenon (concealed mortising).
LXXXVI. Blocking (gluing with use of blocks).
LXXXVII. Mortised blocking.
LXXXVIII. Vertical long sawing (foot sawing).

FUNDAMENTAL SERIES.

To simplify matters throughout these series, the two broadest surfaces of any model will be called the sides; the two smaller surfaces in the direction of its grain, the edges; and the two remaining surfaces, showing the ends of the fibers, will be called the ends. The expression "corners" will refer to the lines in which any surfaces meet. Geometrically speaking, this would be incorrect; but mechanically—that is, in the language of the shop—it is not.

The woods, white birch, cherry, red oak, and white wood, will be abbreviated, W. B., C., R. O., W. W. Their prices are: birch, about $5 per hundred; cherry, $7 per hundred; white wood, $4 to $6. Board measure is twelve inches square (surface measure) and one inch or less in thickness. The woods can be obtained in all thicknesses up to six inches, varying in each case by one fourth of an inch in thickness. The length varies from 12 to 16 feet. Standard lengths are 12, 13, 14, and 16 feet. Special lengths are 18 to 20 feet.

The dimensions will be given in the inch and the metric system. In Sweden the latter is used. On all the drawings, the dimensions are stated in inches. The *full* dimensions do not always appear on the drawings, but they are given in the statements under each drawing.

As the ordinary rule has no smaller dimension than one sixteenth of an inch, each number of millimeters is expressed in the nearest equivalent in inches and sixteenths of inches. The abbreviation cm. represents centimeter.

All models, when finished, are to be smoothed with sand-paper, but only on those parts where the use of it is absolutely necessary.

FUNDAMENTAL SERIES

Fine sand-paper, No. 1, should first be used; then coarse, No. 0 or 00.

The tools are always named in the order in which they are used for the making of the models.

Model No. I. (a).

Kindergarten Pointer of W. B. or C. (Straight Grain).

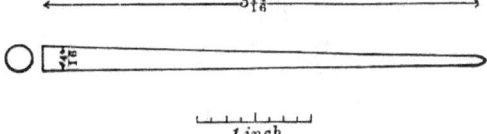

Length, 3⅛ in., or 10 cm. Thickness, 1/10 in., or 0.7 cm.

1. Cut a suitable piece of wood in its entire length, so that two of its surfaces will be at right angles to each other.

2. Cut the required thickness, having first measured same with an inch rule or meter measure.

3. Taper the four sides, having drawn a small square on one of the ends. The object will now have the appearance of a regular four-sided truncated pyramid. Cut the corners, making a regular octagonal truncated pyramid. Cut the corners again, making a regular cone.

4. Measure the required length and cut off at the broad end.

Exercises.—*Long cut and cross cut.*

Model No. I. (b).

Kindergarten Pointer of W. B. or C.

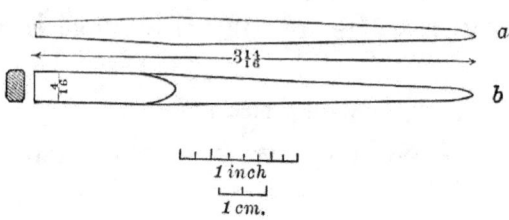

Length, 3 11/16 *in., or* 10 *cm.*   *Thickness*, 4/16 *in., or* 0.7 *cm.*

1. Proceed as in No. I. (*a*), 1, 2, 3.
2. Make the two oblique cuts (the entire work to be done with the Sloyd knife).

Exercises.—*Long cut, cross cut, oblique cut.*

Model No. II.

Rake Tooth of W. B. or C.

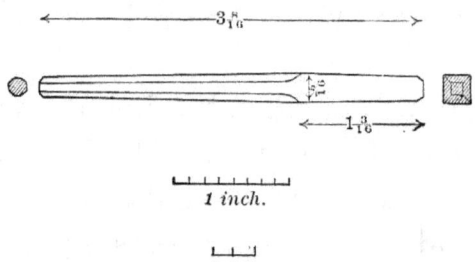

Length, 3 8/16 *in., or* 9 *cm.*   *Thickness*, 5/16 *in., or* 0.8 *cm.*

1. Proceed as in No. I. (*a*), 1 and 2.
2. Taper as in No. I. (*a*), 3, making a regular four-sided truncated pyramid.

FUNDAMENTAL SERIES 105

3. Chamfer the corners, as shown in drawing.
4. Measure the length and cut off.

Exercises.—*Long cut, cross cut, bevel cut.*

Model No. III.

Round Flower Stick of W. W.

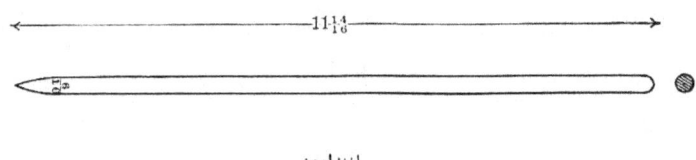

Length, 11¼ *in., or* 30 *cm.*   *Thickness.* ⅜ *in., or* 1 *cm.*

1. Saw off from board with rip saw a suitable piece of wood a little longer than the finished length. Remove this piece with the cross-cut saw.

2. Cut it in its entire length in the form of a square in cross section. Cut the corners, making a regular octagonal prism.

3. Round it to a regular cylinder. Taper the end as shown in drawing. Measure the length and cut off.

4. Round the end as shown in drawing.

Exercises.—*Sawing off, long cut, cross cut, convex cut with knife.*

Model No. IV.

Penholder of W. W.

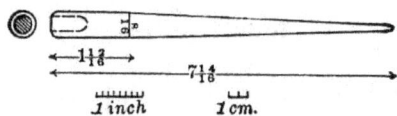

Length, 7¼ in., or 20 cm.   Thickness, ⁹⁄₁₆ in., or 1.3 cm.

1. Proceed as in No. III., 1, 2, 3.

2. Taper as before. Measure the length[1] and cut off.

3. Round the thicker end. The crescent-shaped seat for the pen to fit in is made by boring a series of holes in the lines, as indicated by the drawing, with a suitable twist-drill.

Exercises.—*Sawing off, long cut, cross cut, convex cut.*

---

[1] In laying out the dimensions of a model, it is well to lay the rule down on one of its edges, placing it close to a mark previously drawn on the model from which the required measurement is to be taken. Use the point of the knife to mark out the measurement.

It is likewise advisable to lay out the measurement about one sixteenth of an inch more than the required dimension, so as to have a little spare room to work down on, in case of any slight mistake. By following this rule throughout the series, it will be easier to make the work more correct than if the exact dimension is laid out at the start, either by means of rule, compass, or marking gauge. This also applies to those measurements which of themselves are exceedingly small.

Model No. V.

Rectangular Flower Stick of W. W.

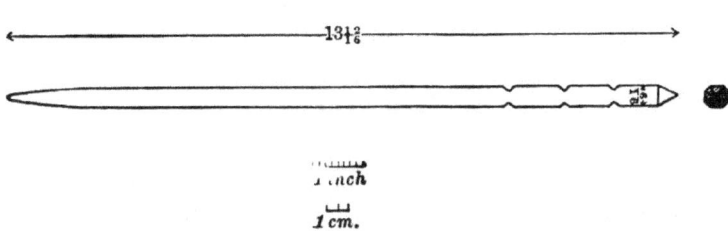

Length, 13⅜ in., or 35 cm.   Thickness, ⅜ in., or 1 cm.

1. Saw off along and across the grain of the board a suitable piece of wood with rip and cross-cut saw.

2. Plane face and edge at right angles with try-plane or fore-plane.

3. Measure the thickness at each end with **rule** and plane down with try-plane.

4. One end is made level with knife. Draw diagonals on it to obtain the point of the pyramid.

5. Mark out the length of the pyramid on the four sides.

6. Cut obliquely to produce pyramid.

7. Measure the entire length and cut off.

Exercises.—*Sawing off, long sawing, edge planing, squaring, oblique cut, convex cut.*

Model No. VI.

Slate-Pencil Holder of W. W.

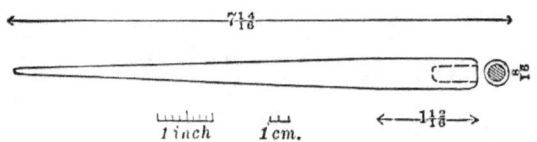

Length, 7 14/16 in., or 20 cm. Thickness, 8/16 in., or 1.3 cm.

1. Remove from block, with rip and cross-cut saw, a suitable piece of wood. Cut as in previous model, making the four sides equal.

2. Square off one end with knife, and draw diagonal lines on this end, so as to locate the center. Bore a hole with suitable bit.

3. Measure the length and cut off.

4. Lay out on the second end the reduced square. Draw lines to indicate the required taper on two opposite sides. Cut to these lines. Now lay out the lines of taper on the two remaining sides and cut to these lines.

5. Reduce to its cylindrical form with knife and half-round file.

6. Round the ends with file.

Exercises.—*Sawing off, long cut, boring with shell-bit, convex cut, cross cut, filing.*

Model No. VII.
Key Label of W. W.

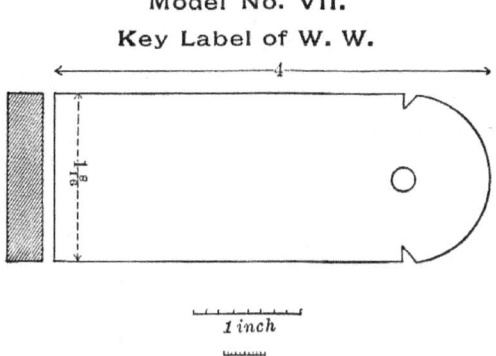

Length, 4 *in., or* 10.1 *cm.*   *Breadth,* 1$\frac{8}{16}$ *in., or* 3.8 *cm.*

1. Prepare the wood as before.

2. Plane face and edge at right angles with try-plane.[1] Gauge breadth and plane down.

3. Draw outlines with pencil, square, and compass.

4. Bore the hole with gouge bit. Gauge thickness and plane down.

5. Saw off the square end with back cross-cut saw and cut the curved end with knife. Finish both ends with half-round file.

6. Cut the notches.

Exercises.—*Sawing off, cross cut, edge planing, squaring, gauging, boring with shell bit, convex cut, cross cut, filing.*

---

[1] Even on surfaces of small area the Swedes use the try-plane, and the Sloyd is taught according to this practice. It is believed that the child will be assisted in his work by the weight of the tool itself. However, a smoothing-plane might be used for such work as this.

Model No. VIII.

Thread Winder of W. B.

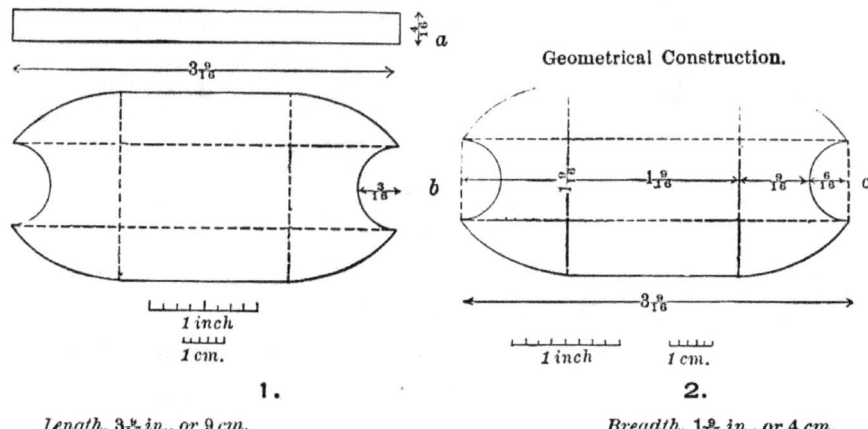

Geometrical Construction.

1. 2.

Length, 3 9/16 in., or 9 cm.   Breadth, 1 9/16 in., or 4 cm.

1. Prepare the wood as before, sawing out a piece about one half an inch longer than the finished length.

2. Plane face and edge at right angles with try-plane.

3. Draw the outline as indicated in the geometrical construction (2), with pencil, square, and compass, allowing equal waste on each end.

4. The concave ends are made by boring with a center-bit.

5. Gauge the thickness and plane down with try-plane.[1]

[1] This object may first be reduced to its required thickness,

FUNDAMENTAL SERIES 111

6. Saw close to the line with a fine compass saw, leaving sufficient material so as to finish to the line with knife and file.

7. Slightly round the concave ends with knife and smooth with file.

8. Smooth the edges with file.

Exercises.—*Sawing off, long sawing, face planing, edge planing, squaring, boring with center-bit, gauging, convex sawing, long cut, convex cut, concave cut, filing.*

Model No. IX.

Dibble of W. W.

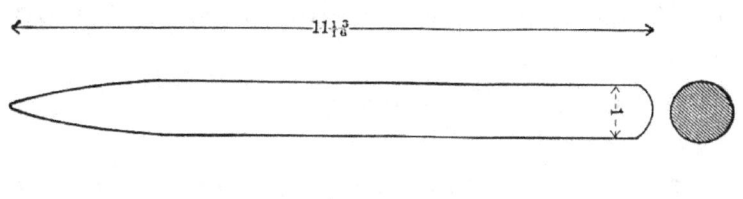

Length, 11⅜ in., or 30 cm.   *Thickness*, 1 in., or 2.5 cm.

1. Prepare the wood as before.[1]

and then fastened to another piece of wood in the vise, and the openings for the concave ends may be carefully bored through from both sides. This, however, is not the "Nääs method."

[1] In removing the wood from the block or board, it is best

2. Plane face and edge at right angles with use of jack and try-plane.

3. Gauge breadth and thickness and then plane down.

4. Draw diagonals on each end and, from the centers thus obtained, describe circles within the given squares.

5. Plane off the corners with try-plane, making the work octagonal. Then make it sixteen sided.

6. Finish to a cylinder with the smoothing-plane.

7. Taper one end with knife.

8. Measure the length and saw off.

9. Round both ends as indicated in the drawing.

10. Smooth with file.

Exercises.—*Sawing off, long sawing, edge planing, squaring, gauging, bevel planing, convex shaping or modeling with the plane, convex cut, cross cut, filing.*

in all cases to take the piece quite a little longer, broader, and thicker than the finished length, breadth, and thickness require, because more accurate results will be obtained by working a model down to its correct dimensions with smoothing tools, such as the file, scraper, or spokeshave, than by depending too much upon the saw or jack-plane. Besides, a slight error can more readily be rectified.

FUNDAMENTAL SERIES

Model No. X.

Harness Pin of W. B.

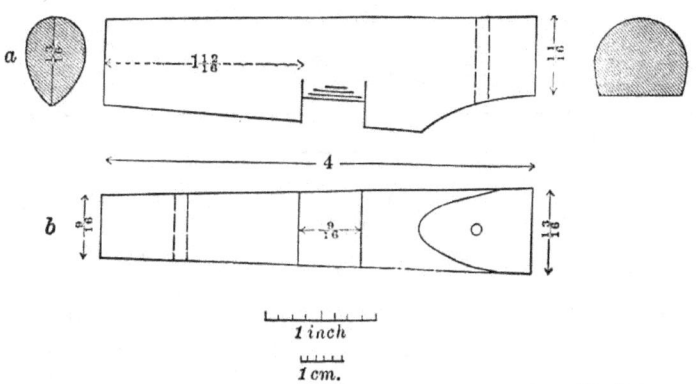

Length, 4 in., or 10 cm.   Breadth, 13/16 in., or 2 cm.

1. Saw off from block as in previous exercises.

2. Dress the piece on its four sides with a small hand ax.

3. Draw the form on each end as indicated in the drawing. Reduce to shape with knife.

4. Locate the position of the recess with compass, and cut out with tenon saw and knife.

5. Bore the holes with a suitable gouge or auger-bit.[1]

6. Smooth with file.

Exercises.—*Sawing off, chopping, long cut, cross sawing with tenon saw, concave cut, boring with shell bit, cross cut, convex cut, filing.*

[1] The boring may be done from both sides.

Model No. XI.

Paper-cutter of W. B.

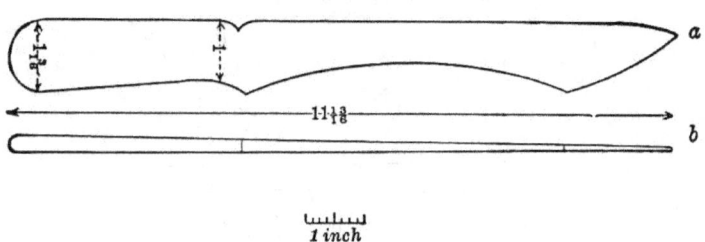

Length, 11 43/48 in., or 30 cm. Breadth, 1 3/16 in., or 3 cm.

1. Saw off from block. Plane one face and edge at right angles with try-plane. Gauge the thickness. First saw off with rip saw and then plane down with try-plane.

2. Draw outline as in drawing.

3. First saw off with compass saw; then smooth the edges with knife.

4. Pare off the broad surfaces from the outline of the back down to a center line (previously drawn). This center line will thus become the cutting edge of the paper-knife.

5. Round the edges of the handle and the back edge of the blade with knife.

6. Smooth with file and scraper.

Exercises.—*Sawing off, long sawing, face planing, edge planing, squaring, gauging, wave sawing, concave cut, convex cut, plane surface cut, filing, scraping.*

Model No. XII. (a).

Movable Pail Handle of W. B.

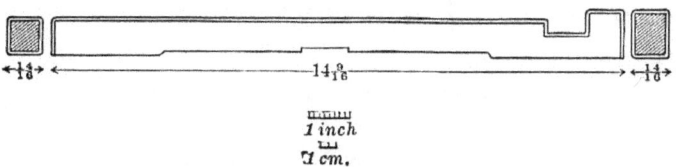

Length, 14 9/16 in., or 37 cm.　　　　　　Breadth, ⅞ in., or 2.2 cm.

1. Prepare the wood as in previous exercises.

2. Plane face and edge at right angles with try-plane. Gauge breadth and thickness and plane down.

3. Draw outline according to the drawing. With the knife proceed to finish the surface adjacent to the recess, a sufficient length to allow the remaining surface to be finished with a try-plane (obstacle planing).

4. Finish the recess and the projection piece with tenon saw, chisel, and knife.

5. Finish the depressions in the lower surface with tenon saw, chisel, and knife, having measured their position by compass, square, and gauge.

6. Measure the length and saw off at right angles with tenon saw. Smooth the ends with chisel.

7. Smooth entire model with file and scraper.

Exercises.—*Sawing off, long sawing, face planing,*

edge planing, squaring, gauging, obstacle planing, perpendicular chiseling, long cut, cross cut, oblique cut, bevel cut, filing, scraping.

Model No. XII. (b).

Part of an Ox-bow[1] of W. B.

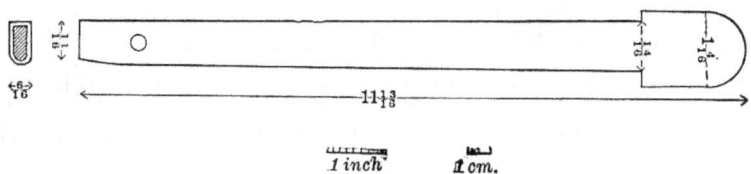

The measurements as given on the drawing are to be doubled in making each piece of the model.

Length, 23⅜ *in., or* 60 *cm.*   *Breadth,* 2⅜ *in., or* 6.35 *cm.*

1. Prepare the wood as in previous exercises.

2. Plane face and edge at right angles with try-plane.

3. Gauge breadth and thickness. Plane down.

4. Draw outlines as in drawing with compass, square, and marking gauge. Bring out the form with rip saw, smoothing-plane, knife, compass saw, and chisel.

5. Mark the position of the hole. Bore with center-bit from both sides.

---

[1] The Swedish ox-bow consists of two pieces of wood such as the model, which are fastened together with a thin iron chain. This is unlike the American ox-bow, which is made of one piece bent in the form of the letter **U**.

edge planing, squaring, gauging, obstacle planing, perpendicular chiseling, long cut, cross cut, oblique cut, bevel cut, filing, scraping.

Model No. XII. (b).

Part of an Ox-bow[1] of W. B.

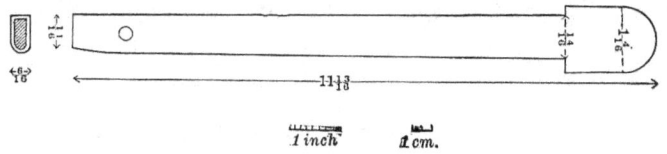

The measurements as given on the drawing are to be doubled in making each piece of the model.

Length, 23⅛ in., or 60 cm.   Breadth, 2⅝ in., or 6.35 cm.

1. Prepare the wood as in previous exercises.

2. Plane face and edge at right angles with try-plane.

3. Gauge breadth and thickness. Plane down.

4. Draw outlines as in drawing with compass, square, and marking gauge. Bring out the form with rip saw, smoothing-plane, knife, compass saw, and chisel.

5. Mark the position of the hole. Bore with center-bit from both sides.

---

[1] The Swedish ox-bow consists of two pieces of wood such as the model, which are fastened together with a thin iron chain. This is unlike the American ox-bow, which is made of one piece bent in the form of the letter **U.**

FUNDAMENTAL SERIES

6. Measure the length and saw off with tenon saw.

7. Finish the edges and ends with chisel, file, and scraper.

Exercises.—*Sawing off, long sawing, face planing, edge planing, squaring, gauging, obstacle planing, convex sawing, perpendicular chiseling, boring with center-bit, convex cut, cross cut, bevel cut, filing, scraping.*

Model No. XIII.

Small Bowl of W. B.

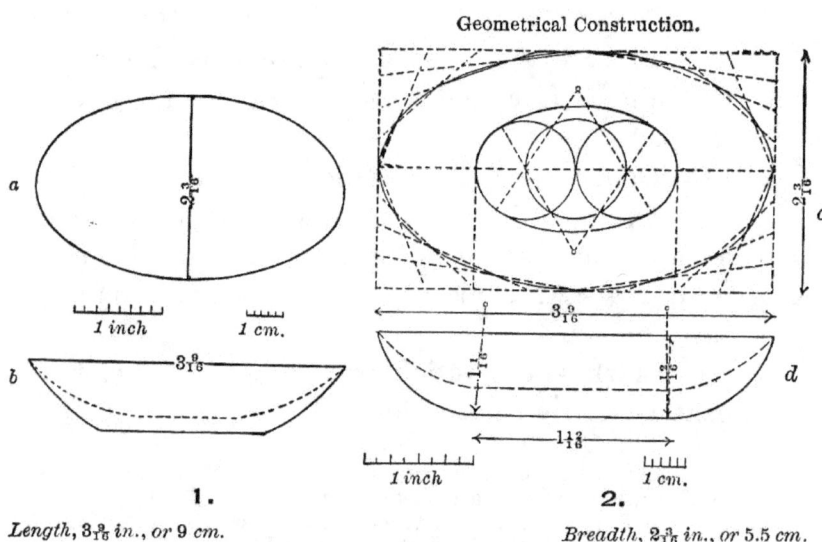

Geometrical Construction.

1.

Length, $3\frac{9}{16}$ *in., or 9 cm.*

2.

Breadth, $2\frac{3}{16}$ *in., or 5.5 cm.*

1. Remove from block as in previous exercises.

2. Plane face and edge at right angles with try-plane.

3. Gauge thickness and plane down.

4. Draw outlines on two opposite sides, according to geometrical construction (2), with try-square and compass.

5. Saw off with frame compass saw,[1] and chisel close to the line.

6. Smooth with file.

7. Proceed to hollow out as indicated by drawing, with gouge and mallet, and finish with spoon-iron or spoon-gouge.

8. Smooth the inside surface with sand-paper.

9. Form the outside surface with chisel, knife, and file.

10. Use the scraper for smoothing all the surfaces.

Exercises.—*Sawing off, long sawing, face planing, edge planing, squaring, gauging, convex sawing, perpendicular chiseling, filing, gouging with gouge and spoon-iron, oblique chiseling, convex cut, scraping.*

---

[1] All Swedish hand saws are frame saws, except the tenon, keyhole, and grooving saws. The latter are small saws. The Swedes prefer the frame saws to either our large rip or our cross-cut saws, claiming that the weight of the frame makes the sawing to a straight line easier. Their dexterity in handling these saws is quite remarkable.

Model No. XIV.

Hammer Handle of W. B.

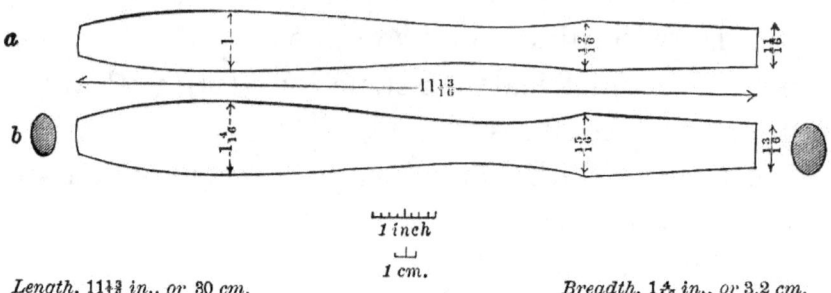

Length, 11⅜ in., or 80 cm.   Breadth, 1¼ in., or 3.2 cm.

1. Remove from block.

2. Plane face and edge at right angles with try-plane.

3. Draw outlines on opposite sides.

4. Saw nearly to these lines with broad frame compass saw, and finish to the lines with spokeshave.

5. Cut away the corners with knife, and finish to elliptical form with spokeshave.

6. Measure the length, and saw off with back saw.

7. Finish with knife. Smooth with file and scraper.

Exercises.—*Sawing off, long sawing, face planing, edge planing, squaring, wave sawing, smoothing with spokeshave, bevel cut, modeling with spokeshave, cross cut, filing, scraping.*

Model No. XV.

Spoon of W. B.

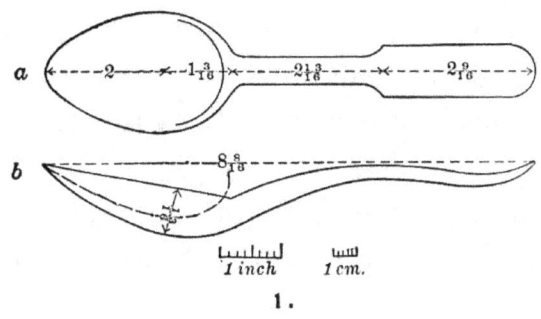

1.

Geometrical Construction.

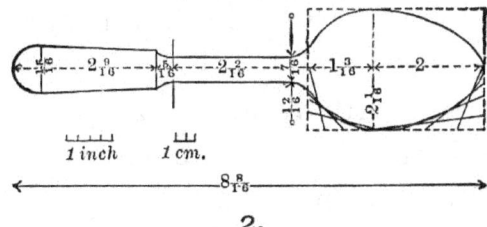

2.

Length, 8 8/16 in., or 21.5 cm.   Breadth, 2 1/16 in., or 5.2 cm.

1. Prepare wood as in previous exercises.

2. Cut away with a small hand ax, so as to obtain approximate width and thickness.

3. Plane face and edge at right angles with jack and try-plane. Gauge a little beyond the required width and plane down.

4. On each edge draw the outline of the upper side of the spoon, as indicated in second drawing

(side view of spoon), by means of try-square and compass.

5. Saw off with rip and compass saw. Smooth with chisel and file.

6. Draw on the surface thus obtained an outline of the upper surface of the model, according to geometrical construction drawing (2), with try-square and compass.

7. Bring out the form of the sides with center-bit[1] and compass saw. Smooth with chisel and file.

8. The hollow is made as in No. XIII. 7.

9. Draw outline of the lower surface of the model.

10. Saw out with compass saw.

11. Finish the entire model with knife and smooth with file and scraper.

Exercises.—*Sawing off, chopping, face planing, edge planing, squaring, gauging, oblique sawing, wave sawing, oblique chiseling, boring with center-bit, convex sawing, perpendicular chiseling, filing, gouging with gouge and spoon-iron, convex cut, concave cut, long cut, scraping.*

[1] In bringing out the form of the sides with the center-bit, it is best to bore from both sides. The opening will then be cleaner. This will also prevent splitting on the lower side.

Model No. XVI.

Chopping Board of W. W.

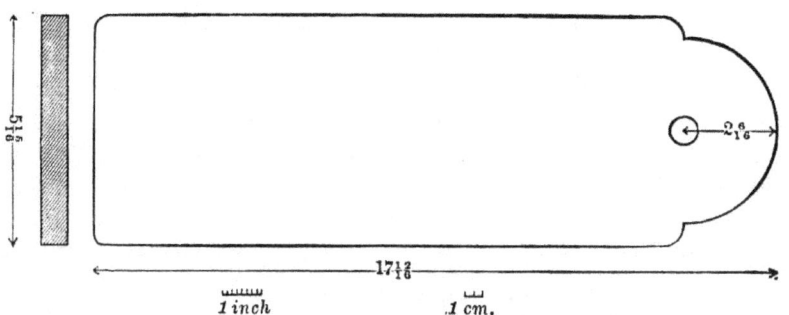

Length, 17¼⅜ *in., or* 45.1 *cm*.   *Breadth*, 5⅛ *in., or* 15.1 *cm*.

1. Prepare the wood as in former exercises.
2. Plane face and edge at right angles with jack and try-plane. Gauge breadth and plane down.
3. Draw outline of the ends with square and compass. Bore the hole with center-bit.
4. Saw off the ends with back cross-cut and frame compass saw. Smooth the ends with chisel, smoothing-plane, and file. Gauge the thickness, and plane down with jack and try-plane.
5. Smooth the sides and edges with smoothing-plane. Finish the edges and ends with scraper.

Exercises.—*Sawing off, face planing, edge planing, squaring, gauging, boring with center-bit, convex sawing, perpendicular chiseling, end planing, filing, smoothing up, scraping.*

Model No. XVII.

Flower-pot Cross of W. W.

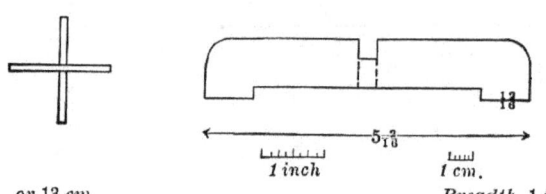

Length, 5 2/16 in., or 13 cm.   Breadth, 1 in., or 2.5 cm.

1. Saw from block a piece of sufficient length for the two parts of the model.

2. Plane face and edge at right angles with jack and try-plane. Gauge breadth and thickness, and plane down with try-plane. Saw into two parts of equal length.

3. Lay out outline on these parts with compass, try-square, and gauge. Draw the recess on one piece at the top, as shown by full lines of the drawing; and on the other, at the bottom, as shown by dotted lines, so that they can be joined in the form of a cross.

4. Lay out outline of curved corners and of feet. Cut recesses, form of feet, and curved corners with knife. Fit together.

Exercises.—*Sawing off, long sawing, edge planing, squaring, gauging, cross cut, long cut, convex cut, filing, halving with knife.*

NÄÄS MODEL SERIES

Model No. XVIII.

Scythe Sharpener of R. O.

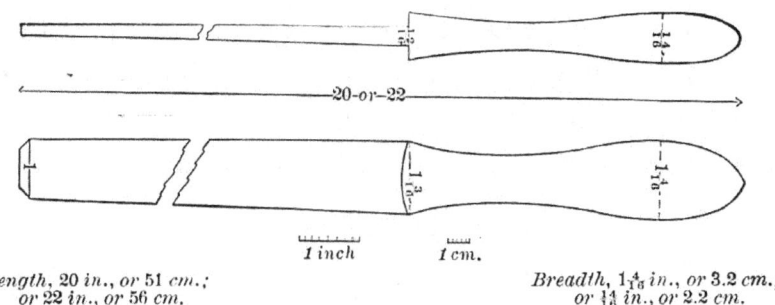

Length, 20 *in.,* or 51 *cm.;*
or 22 *in.,* or 56 *cm.*

Breadth, 1 4/16 *in.,* or 3.2 *cm.;*
or 7/8 *in.,* or 2.2 *cm.*

1. Prepare wood as in former exercises. Plane face and edge at right angles with try-plane. Gauge thickness and plane down.

2. Lay out the outline of the blade with square, rule, and compass. Shape with rip saw, jack-plane, spokeshave, knife, and file.[1]

3. Outline handle[2] with square and compass, and make same with compass saw, knife, and spokeshave.

4. Measure the length, and saw off with tenon saw.

[1] The three files used in the Sloyd work are the flat, the half-round, and the round file. The flat is used on plane surfaces, the half-round on plane and curved surfaces, and the full round in holes or curved openings.

[2] In making the handle, a center line may be drawn, and a cardboard templet may be employed. Templets are not used in the Nääs method.

5. Smooth the handle with flat file and scraper, and the edges of the blade with file.

Exercises.—*Sawing off, long sawing, face planing, edge planing, squaring, gauging, obstacle planing, smoothing with spokeshave, wave sawing, modeling with spokeshave, concave cut, convex cut, cross cut, oblique cut, filing, scraping, working in hard wood.*

Model No. XIX.

Scoop of B.

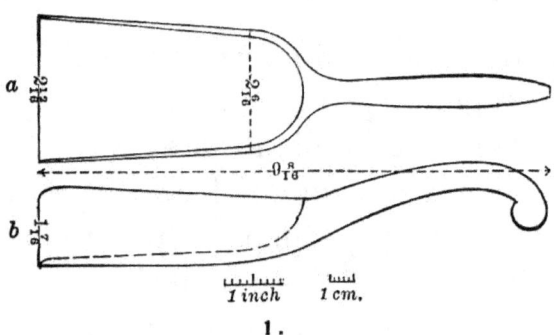

1.

Geometrical Construction.

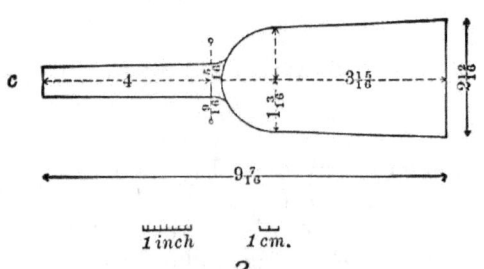

2.

Length, $9\frac{7}{16}$ in., or 24 cm.   *Breadth*, $2\frac{12}{16}$ in., or 7 cm.

1. Prepare wood as before. Reduce it to

approximate size with hand ax. Plane face and edge at right angles with jack and try-plane.

2. Construct diagram of model as in drawing 1 (*a*) with try-square and compass.

3. Make the form with center-bit, rip saw, and frame compass saw. Smooth with smoothing-plane and chisel.

4. Construct diagram as in drawing 1 (*b*). Saw with rip and compass saw to bring out the form. Smooth with smoothing-plane and chisel.

5. The hollow is outlined with compass and gauge, and is made with gouge, mallet, spoon-iron or spoon-gouge, file, and scraper.

6. Produce the form of the lower surface of the model with hand ax,[1] smoothing-plane, and knife. Smooth the entire model with file and scraper.

Exercises.—*Sawing off, chopping, face planing, squaring, boring with center-bit, long sawing, convex sawing, perpendicular chiseling, oblique sawing, oblique planing (tapering), oblique chiseling, gouging with gouge and spoon-iron, filing, modeling with plane, convex cut, concave cut, cross cut, scraping.*

[1] The hand ax is a tool not used by us for this purpose. We would take a chisel instead; but the correct use of the hand ax is very important, and it will be found advisable not to substitute the chisel for it in the Sloyd work.

Model No. XX.

Clothes Rack of W. W.

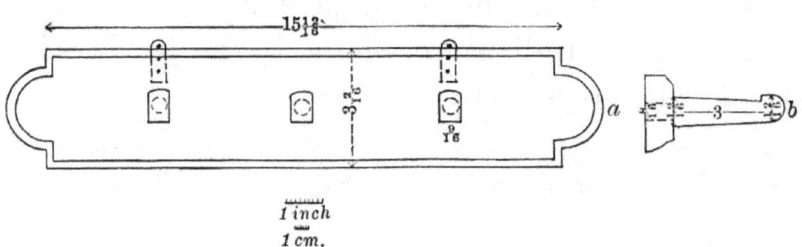

Length, 15⅝ in., or 40 cm.   Breadth, 3²⁄₁₆ in., or 8 cm.

1. Saw out a suitable piece of wood for the flat portion of the model.

2. Plane face and edge at right angles with jack and try-plane. Gauge breadth and plane down.

3. Draw a center line the whole length of this piece, on which locate the position of the three holes for the pegs to be fitted in, and also locate the centers for the semicircular ends.

4. With center-bit, carefully bore these holes at right angles to the surface of the plate.

5. Outline diagram of the flat portion or plate of the model as in drawing (*a*). Shape with frame compass saw, chisel, and file. Gauge thickness, and plane down with try-plane.

6. Measure the required width of the chamfers, and mark same with gauge. Chamfer with try-plane, knife, file, and scraper.

7. Plane the wood for the pegs in one piece with try-plane. Gauge width and thickness and plane down. Measure the length of each peg about half an inch longer than the required length, and saw off at right angles with tenon saw.

8. Draw diagonals on one end of each peg. With the same center-bit [1] with which the holes in the plate of the model were bored, and with the intersection of each two of these diagonals as a center, describe a circumference.

9. Draw outline of each peg as in drawing (*b*), measuring the exact length from the semicircular end of each peg to the shoulder, so as to give the extra half-inch to the length of the peg that is to project through the plate.

10. Make the pegs with tenon saw, chisel, knife, and file. Glue the pegs in position as indicated in the drawing, so that they are at right angles to the plate, being careful that the hook in each peg-head is nearest to the top edge of the plate.

11. Dress off the ends of the pegs that project through the rear of the plate with chisel and smoothing-plane.

---

[1] A compass may also be used for this purpose.

FUNDAMENTAL SERIES

12. Take a small piece of flat iron suitable for the hangers. Fold same together at the middle. File the ends into the shape indicated by the drawing. Make the holes with stamp and hammer. Fasten in position with wood-screws.

13. Smooth the entire model with scraper.

Exercises.— *Sawing off, long sawing, face planing, edge planing, squaring, gauging, boring with center-bit, convex sawing, perpendicular chiseling, filing, oblique beveling, bevel cut, cross cut, convex cut, fitting in pegs, smoothing up, oblique chiseling, gluing, sinking iron plates, scraping.*

Model No. XXI.

Flower-pot Stand of W. W.

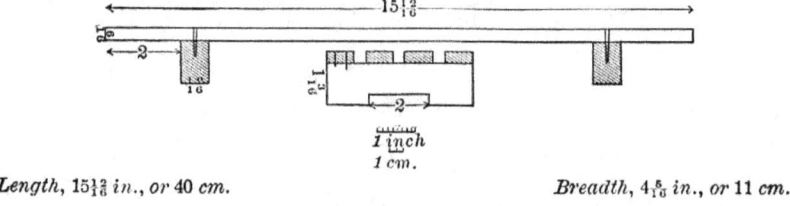

Length, 15¹³⁄₁₆ in., or 40 cm. Breadth, 4⁵⁄₁₆ in., or 11 cm.

1. Saw off from board a suitable piece for the strips.

2. Plane face and edge at right angles with jack and try-plane.

3. Gauge thickness and plane down.

4. Measure the length, and saw off with tenon saw. Smooth the ends in shooting-board with try-plane.

5. Mark the width of each strip at each end, and connect the points obtained with penciled lines, leaving sufficient space between the lines to saw and dress.

6. Saw out the strips with rip saw, and plane to required width with try-plane.

7. Saw out a suitable piece of wood sufficient for the two legs. Plane face and edge at right angles with try-plane.

8. Gauge breadth and thickness and plane down. Saw in two equal parts with tenon saw.

9. Screw the two pieces in the vise, and smooth the ends with smoothing-plane.

10. Draw outline of legs with compass, try-square, and gauge, and work the pieces to the lines with tenon saw, chisel, knife, and file.

11. Nail down the strips at right angles to the legs with suitable brad-head nails. Drive the nails below the surface of the wood with nail-set and hammer.[1]

---

[1] Wherever it is possible, each nail should be driven into the wood in a slightly inclined direction, and always in the opposite direction to that in which the preceding nail has been driven in. This will make the work hold together better.

FUNDAMENTAL SERIES 131

12. Smooth the ends of the strips with file, and the entire model with scraper.

Exercises.—*Sawing off, long sawing, face planing, edge planing, squaring, gauging, end planing, cross sawing with tenon-saw, cross cut, long cut, filing, nailing, punching nails, smoothing up.*

Model No. XXII.

Ax Handle of W. B.

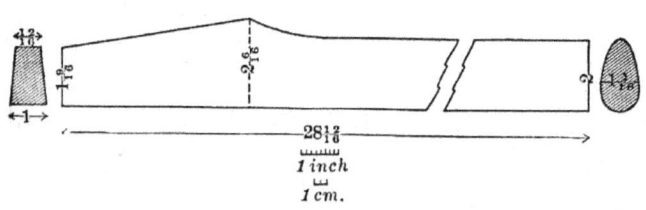

Length, 28⅔ in., or 73 cm.   Breadth, 2⅜ in., or 6 cm.

1. Saw off from block with rip and cross-cut saw. Dress to approximate thickness with hand ax. Plane face and edge at right angles with jack and try-plane. Gauge thickness and plane down.

2. Outline diagram as in drawing and saw off with rip and frame compass saw.

3. Cut the edges with drawing-knife.

4. Shape with smoothing-plane, spokeshave, and knife. Measure the length, and saw off with cross-cut saw. Smooth with file and scraper.

Exercises. — *Sawing off, chopping, face planing, edge planing, squaring, gauging, long sawing, convex sawing, beveling with draw-knife, modeling with plane, modeling with spokeshave, oblique planing, concave cut, bevel cut, filing, scraping.*

Model No. XXIII.

Footstool of W. W.

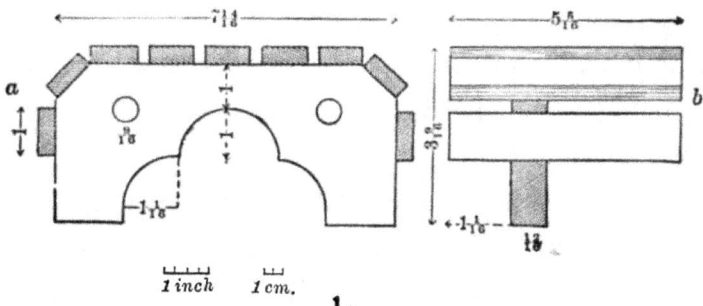

1.

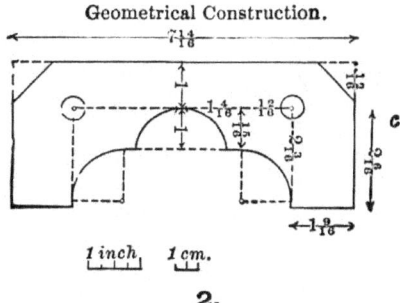

2.

Length, 10¹⁸⁄₁₆ *in., or* 27 *cm.*   *Breadth,* 8¹⁰⁄₁₆ *in., or* 22 *cm.*

1. Make the strips in the same way as in Model No. XXI. 1, 2, 3, 4, 5, 6.

2. Saw out from board a piece of sufficient length for the two legs.

3. Plane face and edge at right angles with jack and try-plane.

4. Gauge the breadth and plane down.

5. Saw at right angles into two equal parts with tenon saw.

6. Nail the two parts together. Smooth the ends with smoothing-plane.

7. Outline diagram as in geometrical construction (drawing on both sides) with try-square and compass.

8. Bring out the form with tenon saw, compass saw, chisel, center-bit, gouge and file.

9. Take the legs apart, gauge the thickness of each, and plane down with jack and try-plane.

10. Nail down the strips, driving the nails below the surface of the wood with nail-set and hammer.

11. Smooth the ends of the strips with file, and the entire model with scraper.

Exercises.—*Sawing off, long sawing, face planing, edge planing, squaring, gauging, end planing, convex sawing, perpendicular gouging, oblique sawing, oblique chiseling, boring with center-bit, filing, smoothing up, nailing, punching in nails.*

Model No. XXIV.

Barrel Cover of W. W.

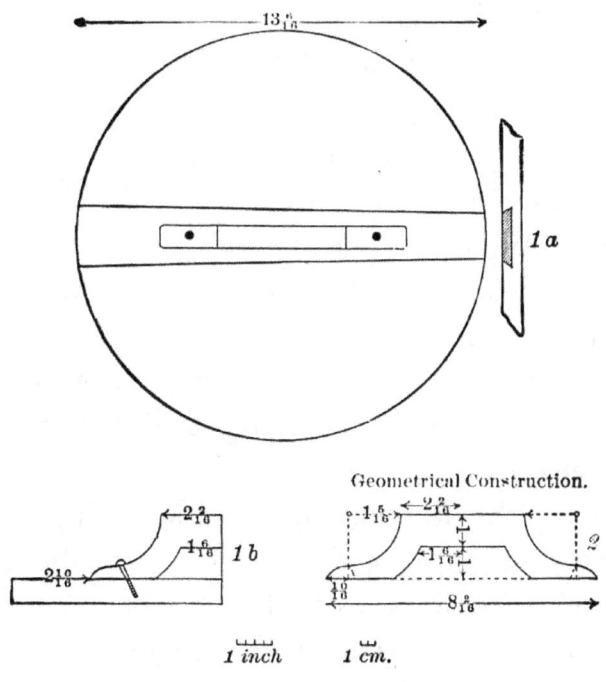

Diameter, 13 8/10 in., or 34 cm.

1. Saw off from block with rip and cross-cut saw two pieces of equal size, which, when put together and dressed, will form the completed disk.[1]

2. Plane face and edge of each piece at right

[1] The disk may be made either of two or of three pieces glued together, as may be found preferable.

angles, taking especial care to plane the edges very smooth, as the pieces are now to be glued together. While drying, clamp these pieces in the vise or otherwise.[1]

3. After the glue has dried, dress off the entire surface to a true plane.

4. Outline diagram as in drawing 1 (*a*) with compass and rule.

5. Lay out the position of the grooving in which the dovetailed tongue is to be fitted with try-square, compass, rule, and marking awl.[2] Gauge the depth of the grooving. Remove so as to produce the groove, using knife, tenon saw, chisel, and router.

6. Make the dovetailed tongue, being careful to plane same to a width which is to be a little more than the width of the groove. The sides of the tongue incline in the form of a wedge, and its depth in the form of a dovetail.

7. Fit the tongue into the groove and glue it tightly in position. Plane down the projecting surface of the tongue flush with the surface of the disk.

---

[1] It requires three to four hours for the glue to harden.
[2] The object of this dovetailed tongue is to make the cover stronger, and to prevent it from warping. The grooving is laid out in the opposite direction to the grain of the wood.

8. Gauge the thickness of the disk and plane down with jack and try-plane.

9. The circular form is made with frame compass saw. Smooth the edge and bring out the form with spokeshave and file.

10. Smooth the sides with smoothing-plane.

11. Saw out with rip saw a small piece of white birch suitable for the handle. Gauge the required breadth and thickness, and plane down with try-plane.

12. Outline diagram of the handle as in geometrical construction (2) with try-square and compass.

13. Bring out the form with rip saw, chisel, smoothing-plane, knife, file, and scraper.

14. As shown in drawing, the holes for the screws are to be bored at a slight inclination, with a suitable bit. Screw the handle in place.

15. Finish entire model with scraper.

Exercises.—*Sawing off, face planing, plane jointing, squaring, gluing, dovetail clamping, gauging, circular sawing, smoothing with spokeshave, modeling with spokeshave, filing, long sawing, convex sawing, perpendicular chiseling, concave chiseling, modeling with plane, long cut, bevel cut, boring with shell-bit, scraping, fixing with screws.*

Model No. XXV.

Box of W. W.

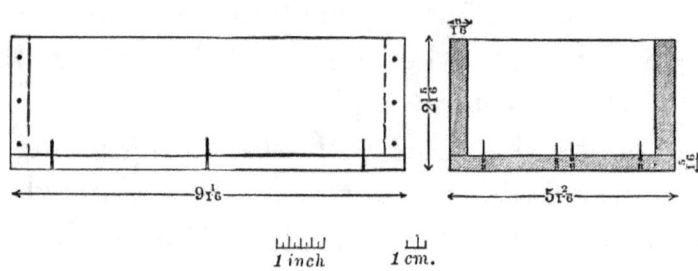

Length, 9 1/16 in., or 23 cm.   Breadth, 5 2/16 in., or 13 cm.

1. Saw out with rip saw two pieces, each of sufficient length to make one long and one short side.

2. Plane face and edge of each at right angles with try-plane. Gauge width and thickness and plane down.

3. Measure the length of each side and each end with ruler and try-square, and saw off at right angles with tenon-saw.

4. Smooth the ends of each of the four pieces in shooting-board with try-plane.

5. Nail the parts together with brad nails, having bored holes with brad-awl. Drive the nails below the surface, using a nail-set and hammer.

6. Smooth the lower edges of the sides and ends with smoothing-plane.

7. Saw out a suitable piece for the bottom of the box.

8. Plane face and edge at right angles.

9. Gauge width and thickness, and plane down.

10. With rule and try-square, lay off the length one fourth of an inch longer than the finished length.

11. Saw off at right angles with tenon saw.

12. Nail down the bottom of the box, being careful that the box is square before completing the nailing.[1]

13. Smooth the entire model with smoothing-plane and scraper.

Exercises.—*Sawing off, long sawing, face planing, edge planing, squaring, gauging, planing with shooting-board, nailing, punching in nails, smoothing up, scraping.*

---

[1] In nailing it is well to drive in the nails at the opposite ends first, and those in between afterwards. This, in a measure, prevents the piece from slipping out of position while fastening the parts together.

The nails which are used in the Sloyd work are thin brad nails about an inch and a half long. The common cut nails would not do as well for this work, because it is frequently necessary to drive nails into very thin material, which would be apt to split if rectangular nails were used. If brad nails cannot be obtained, the heads of other round nails should be flattened with a hammer.

Model No. XXVI.

Ladle of W. B.

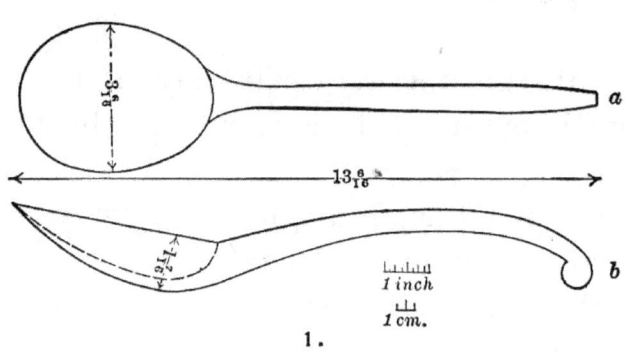

1.

Geometrical Construction.

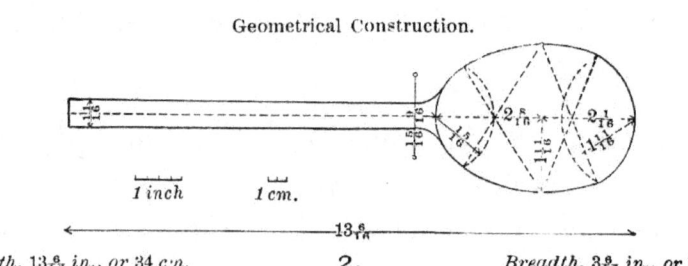

Length, 13 6/16 in., or 34 c:n.   2.   Breadth, 3 6/16 in., or 8.6 cm.

1. Saw off a suitable piece of wood from the block. Cut it with hand ax to approximate thickness.

2. Plane face and edge at right angles with try-plane.

3. Gauge the breadth one fourth of an inch more than the required dimension. Plane down with try-plane.

4. Construct on both side surfaces an outline of the upper surface of the model, as shown in upper part of drawing 1 (*b*). Saw out with rip and frame compass saw. Smooth with smoothing-plane and chisel.

5. Outline diagram as in geometrical construction (2), with rule and compass.

6. Bring out the form with center-bit, rip and compass saw.

7. Smooth with chisel and file.

8. The hollow is made with gouge, mallet, spoon-iron or spoon-gouge, scraper, and sandpaper.

9. Construct outline of the lower surface as in drawing 1 (*b*).

10. Bring out the form with drawing-knife, spokeshave, and knife.

11. Smooth the entire model with file and scraper.

Exercises.—*Sawing off, chopping, face planing, squaring, gauging, oblique sawing, convex sawing, oblique planing, oblique chiseling, boring with center-bit, perpendicular chiseling, gouging with gouge and spoon-iron, wave sawing, modeling with draw-knife, modeling with spokeshave, long cut, convex cut, concave cut, filing, scraping.*

Model No. XXVII.

Baker's Shovel of W. W. or Pine.

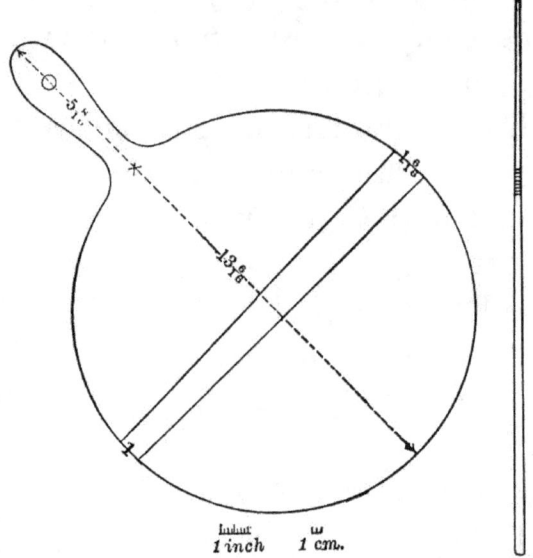

Length, 18¼ in., or 48 cm.   Breadth, 13⅜ in., or 34 cm.

1. Proceed as in Model No. XXIV. 1, 2, 3.

2. Outline diagram as in above drawing.

3. Proceed as in Model No. XXIV. 5, 6, 7, 8. The form is made with frame compass saw. Bore the hole with center-bit.

4. Plane down to an inclined surface with try-plane (square planing across the grain), and afterward with smoothing-plane (wedge planing with smoothing-plane).

5. Smooth the edges with spokeshave, knife, and file.

6. Smooth entire model with scraper.

Exercises.—*Sawing off, chopping, face planing, plain jointing, squaring, gluing, wave sawing, dovetail clamping, boring with center-bit, gauging, smoothing with spokeshave, concave cut, convex cut, square planing across the grain, wedge planing with smoothing plane, modeling with spokeshave, filing, scraping.*

Model No. XXVIII.

Clothes-beater of W. B. or Alder.

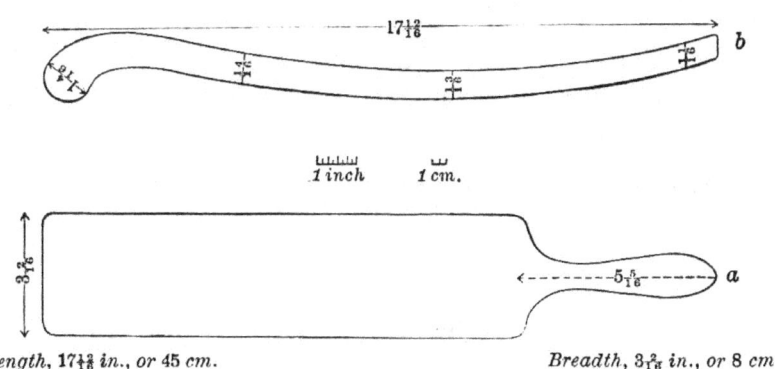

Length, $17\frac{12}{16}$ in., or 45 cm.   Breadth, $3\frac{2}{16}$ in., or 8 cm.

1. Prepare wood as in previous exercises. Dress to approximate thickness with hand ax.

2. Plane face and edge at right angles with jack and try-plane. Gauge breadth and plane down.

3. Outline diagram as in drawing (*b*) on opposite edges. Saw out nearly to these lines with frame compass saw.

4. Plane down the concave surface with compass or circular plane, and the convex surface with smoothing-plane.

5. Outline diagram of the handle with try-square and compass. Saw out with compass saw, and shape with knife and spokeshave.

6. Measure the length, and saw off at right angles with cross-cut saw. Smooth the broad end surface with smoothing-plane and chisel.

7. Round the edges with spokeshave. Smooth with file and scraper.

Exercises.—*Sawing off, chopping, face planing, squaring, gauging, convex sawing, planing with round plane, smoothing up, concave cut, convex cut, end planing, modeling with spokeshave, filing, scraping.*

Model No. XXIX.

Ruler of W. B.

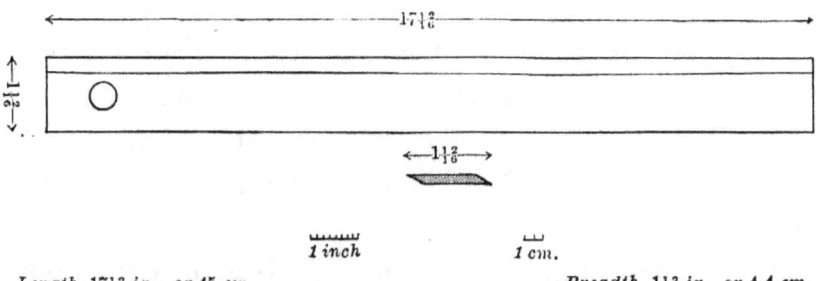

Length, 17⅞ in., or 45 cm.   *Breadth, 1⅜ in., or 4.4 cm.*

1. Prepare wood as in previous exercises.

Plane face and edge at right angles with try-plane.

2. Gauge the breadth and plane down.

3. Mark out the position of the hole with compass, and bore same with center-bit. Gauge the thickness, and saw off with rip saw.

4. As the model piece is now too thin to be held in the iron pins of the bench, it must be fixed with wooden pegs on a perfectly level foundation piece. This foundation piece is to be at least an inch broader than the model piece. The model piece is fixed by boring with a pin-bit through it into the foundation piece about an inch on each side beyond the required length. Two pegs are fitted in to hold the model piece in position.

5. Plane down to required thickness. The bevel on either side is made with try-plane.

6. Measure the length and saw off at right angles with tenon saw. Smooth the ends with knife and file.

Exercises.—*Sawing off, long sawing, face planing, edge planing, squaring, gauging, boring with center-bit, boring with shell-bit, fixing with wooden pegs (for planing thin wood), beveling obliquely, cross cut, filing, scraping.*

Model No. XXX.

Bootjack of W. B.; Foot of W. W.

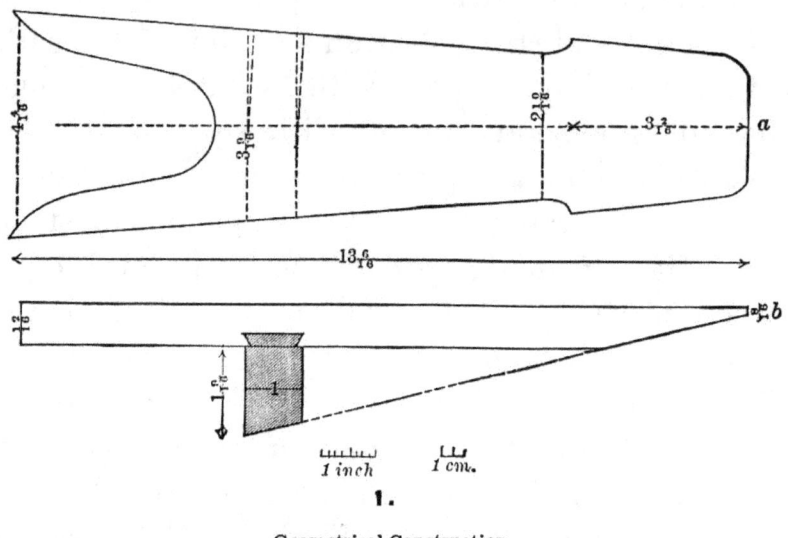

1.

Geometrical Construction.

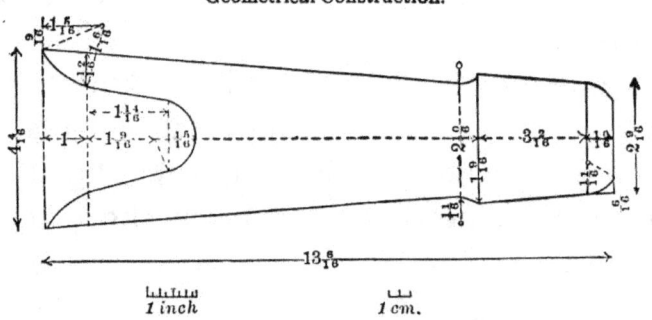

2.

Length, $13\frac{6}{16}$ in., or 34 cm.   Breadth, $4\frac{4}{16}$ in., or 10.8 cm.

1. Saw from block a suitable piece of wood with rip saw. Plane face and edge at right angles with jack and try-plane.

2. Outline diagram as in drawing No. 1 (a) with try-square and compass. Dimensions are to be measured from a center line drawn the entire length of the wood. Saw out with rip and compass saw. Gauge the thickness, and plane down with try-plane.

3. Smooth the edges with spokeshave and chisel.

4. Saw out with rip saw a small piece of W. W. for the foot. Plane face and edge at right angles. Gauge thickness and plane down.

5. Mark out the position of the grooving with compass, marking awl, try-square, bevel, and marking gauge. Remove so as to make the groove with knife, tenon saw, and chisel.

6. Make the dovetailed tongue of the foot, using marking gauge, bevel, and knife. Fit the foot into the groove and glue it fast, driving it in firmly.

7. Saw off with tenon saw the projecting ends of the foot. Smooth with smoothing-plane. Finish the edges with spokeshave, file, and scraper.

8. Lay out the lines on each edge, indicating the inclination of the lower surface of the foot and body with pencil and rule. Finish to these lines with tenon saw and smoothing-plane.

FUNDAMENTAL SERIES 147

9. Round the corners with spokeshave, knife, and file. Smooth with scraper.

Exercises.—*Sawing off, long sawing, face planing, edge planing, squaring, oblique sawing, convex sawing, gauging, smoothing with spokeshave, concave chiseling, straight edge grooving, gluing, end planing, oblique planing, modeling with spokeshave, concave cut, convex cut, cross cut, filing, scraping.*

Model No. XXXI.
Lamp Bracket of W. W.

Geometrical Construction.

Length, $9\frac{4}{8}$ in., or 25 cm.

Breadth, $4\frac{12}{16}$ in., or 12 cm.

1.   2.

1. Saw out a piece of wood of sufficient size for the back and bottom. Plane face and edge of each at right angles.

2. Gauge breadth and thickness and plane down. Measure the length of each, and saw off with tenon saw.

3. Smooth the end surfaces in shooting board with try-plane.

4. The back and the bottom piece are now to be dovetailed together. Lay out the mortises on the back piece as in drawing 1 (b), using compass, rule, and bevel. Mark out the depth of the mortises equal to the thickness of the wood. Make the mortises with tenon saw, chisel, and mallet.

5. Outline diagram of the tenons on the bottom piece by tracing each mortise on one of the end surfaces of the bottom piece with marking awl or knife.

6. Make the length of the tenons equal to thickness of the wood, and mark this out with pencil and try-square.

7. Make the tenons with tenon saw, chisel, and mallet.

8. Outline diagram of the back piece as in geometrical construction (2), with compass and try-square..

9. Saw out with compass saw. Smooth with knife and file.

10. Bore the holes in the back piece, the larger

one with center-bit, and the smaller with brad-awl.

11. Measure the length of the bottom, and saw off with tenon saw. Smooth the edges in shooting-board.

12. Smooth the inner surface of the back and bottom with smoothing-plane. Carefully fit mortises, using the knife, and glue the back and bottom together.

13. Saw out in one length the three side pieces that form the rim of the box of the bracket. Plane face and edge at right angles. Gauge breadth and thickness and plane down.

14. Saw into three equal parts. Smooth the ends in shooting-board.

15. Outline diagram of each, and make with knife. Smooth with file. Nail down to the back and bottom.

16. Smooth all outer surfaces with knife, smoothing-plane, and scraper.

Exercises.—*Sawing off, long sawing, face planing, edge planing, squaring, gauging, planing in shooting-board, common dovetailing, convex sawing, concave cut, long cut, convex cut, cross cut, filing, boring with center-bit, boring with brad-awl, gluing, nailing, punching in nails, smoothing up, scraping.*

Model No. XXXII.

Weaving Shuttle of W. B.

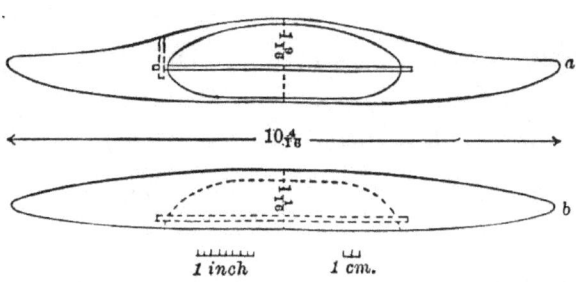

Length, 10 4/16 in., or 26 cm.   Breadth, 1 9/16 in., or 4 cm.

1. Saw off from block a suitable piece of wood somewhat larger than the model. Plane face and edge at right angles with try-plane.

2. Draw outline as shown in drawing (*a*). Saw out with frame compass saw. Smooth the edges with spokeshave and chisel.

3. The position of the hollow is outlined with compass. The hollow is made with outside gouge and mallet. Smooth with sandpaper.

4. Gauge thickness and plane down with try-plane.

5. Outline diagram as in drawing (*b*) on both edges. Saw out with compass saw, and smooth with spokeshave and knife.

6. Make the axle of the bobbin with knife.

FUNDAMENTAL SERIES

Fit same into the hollow with brad-awl and chisel.

7. Smooth entire model with file and scraper.

Exercises.—*Sawing off, long sawing, face planing, edge planing, squaring, convex sawing, smoothing with spokeshave, perpendicular chiseling, scooping with outside gouge, gauging, convex cut, long cut, boring with brad-awl, fitting axle (shuttle), filing, scraping.*

Model No. XXXIII.

Knife Box of W. W.

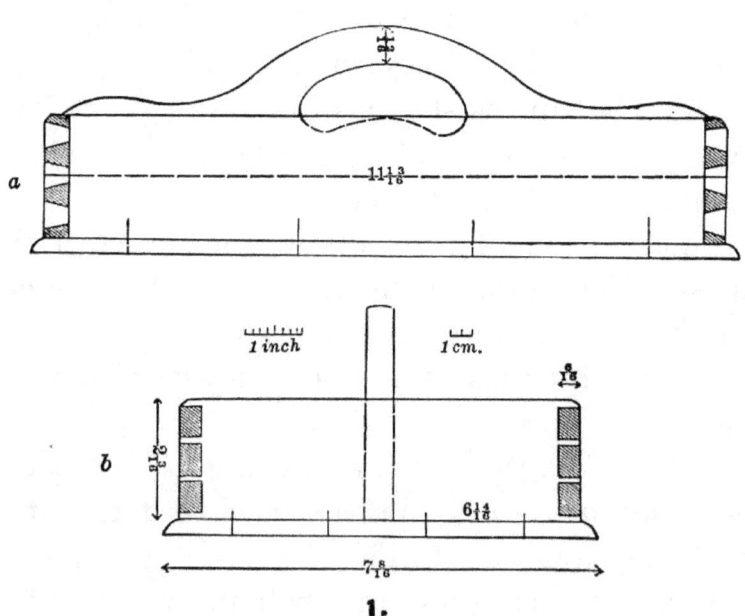

1.

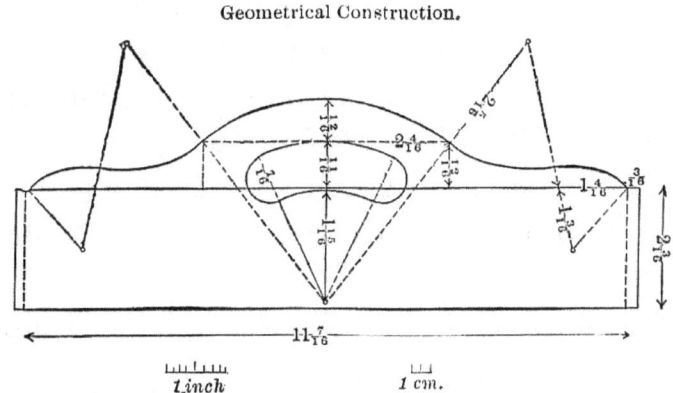

Geometrical Construction.

Length, 11⅜ in., or 30 cm.   2.   Breadth, 7½ in., or 19 cm.

1. Saw out with rip saw two pieces of wood, each of sufficient length for one long and one short side of the box. Plane face and edge at right angles. Gauge the required width and thickness and plane down. Measure the length of each piece, and saw off at right angles with tenon saw. Smooth the edges and ends in shooting-board with try-plane.

2. Mark out the position of the grooving in which the handle is to fit on the inner surface of the two short side pieces, with compass, try-square, and marking gauge. Make the groove with knife and chisel.

3. Make the dovetailing as in Model No. XXXI. 4, 5, 6, 7. After smoothing the inner surfaces of the four parts, glue these together.

4. Saw out a suitable piece for the handle. Plane face and edge at right angles. Gauge breadth and thickness and plane down.

5. Outline diagram of handle as in geometrical construction (2), with try-square and compass. Make the handle with center-bit, compass saw, knife, and file. Smooth the ends in shooting-board with try-plane.

6. Finish the outside of box with smoothing-plane.

7. Fit the handle into the grooving (housing or square grooving), using the smoothing-plane and knife.

8. Saw out a suitable piece for the bottom. Plane face and edge at right angles. Gauge breadth and thickness and plane down. Measure the length, and saw off at right angles with tenon saw.

9. Make the convex edges and ends of the bottom with smoothing-plane and file.

10. Nail down the bottom with brad nails, driving the nails below the surface of the wood.

11. Smooth the entire model with file and scraper.

Exercises.—*Sawing off, long sawing, face planing, edge planing, squaring, gauging, planing in shooting-board, common dovetailing, housing or square* *grooving, gluing, boring with center-bit, wave sawing, convex cut, concave cut, cross cut, long cut, filing, plain jointing, smoothing up, modeling with plane, nailing, punching in nails, scraping.*

Model No. XXXIV.

American Ax Handle of R. O.

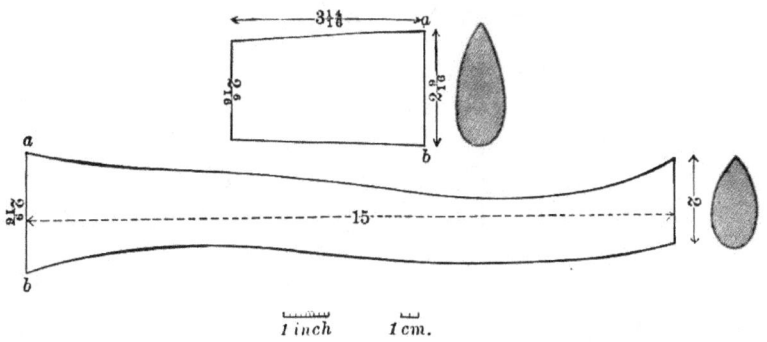

Length, 18⅞ *in., or* 48 *cm.*　　　　　*Breadth,* 2⁹⁄₁₆ *in., or* 6.5 *cm.*

1. Saw out from block a suitable piece of wood with rip saw. Plane face and edge at right angles.

2. Outline diagram as in drawing above, and saw out with frame compass saw.

3. Gauge thickness and plane down.

4. Round the edges with drawing-knife, and shape with spokeshave.

5. Outline diagram of the end surfaces, and form to the same, using drawing-knife, spokeshave, and smoothing-plane.

FUNDAMENTAL SERIES

6. Measure length, and saw off at right angles with tenon saw. Smooth with file and scraper.

Exercises.—*Sawing off, wave sawing, face planing, gauging, smoothing with spokeshave, beveling with draw-knife, modeling with spokeshave, modeling with plane, filing, scraping, working in hard wood.*

Model No. XXXV.
Match Box of W. B.

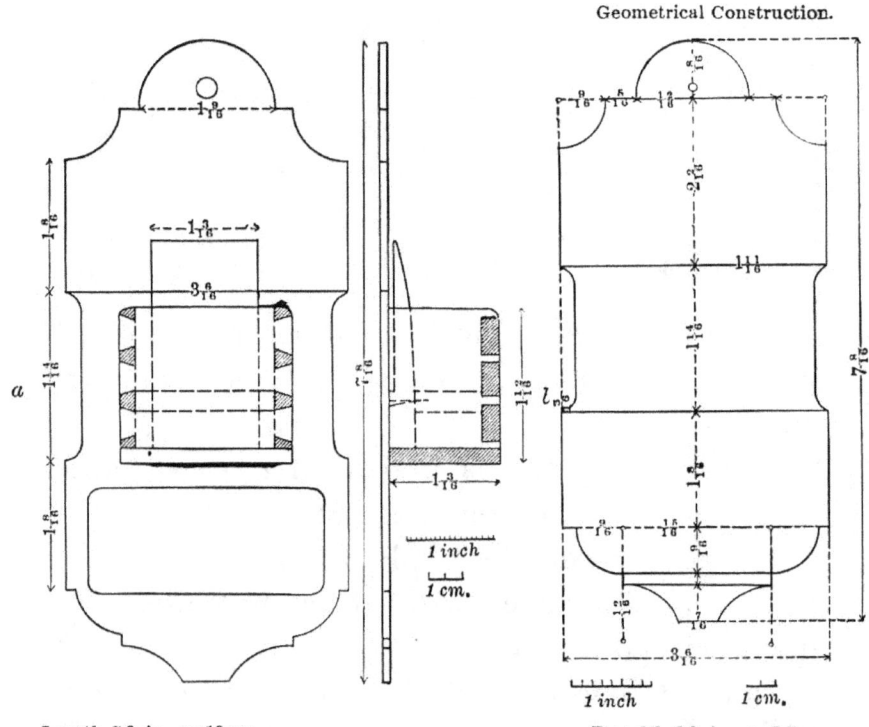

Length, $7\frac{8}{16}$ in., or 19 cm.   Breadth, $3\frac{6}{16}$ in., or 8.5 cm.

1. Saw out the several parts with rip and cross-

cut saw. Plane face and edge of each at right angles with try-plane. Gauge breadth and thickness of each part, and plane down. (The back or wall piece when planed down is adjusted with wooden pegs to a foundation piece, as in Model No. XXIX.)

2. Outline diagram of wall piece as in geometrical construction (2) with try-square and compass. Shape same with knife. Smooth with file.

3. Bore holes with center-bit and brad-awl.

4. Make the dovetailing as in Model No. XXXI.

5. After the lower edges of the box have been smoothed with file, the bottom is glued fast, and held in clamps in position to dry.

6. The box is rounded with knife, and smoothed with file and scraper. Nail down the wall piece.

7. A piece of emery or fine sandpaper may be glued on the front surface of the wall piece, near the lower end, as indicated by the lines on the drawing.

Exercises.—*Sawing off, long sawing, face planing, edge planing, squaring, gauging, planing with round or compass plane, boring with center-bit, concave cut,* *long cut, cross cut, convex cut, filing, planing in shooting-board, common dovetailing, gluing with use of clamps, nailing, boring with brad-awl, scraping.*

Model No. XXXVI.

Baseball Bat of W. B.

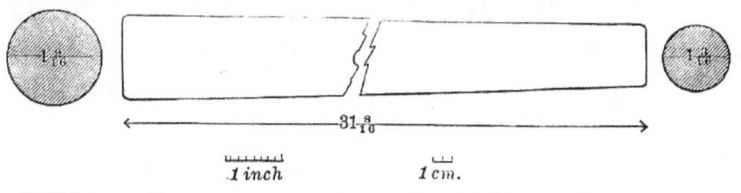

Length, $31\frac{8}{10}$ in., or 80 cm.   Breadth, $1\frac{3}{10}$ in. or $1\frac{9}{10}$ in. ; or 3 or 4 cm.

1. Saw off from block a suitable piece of wood. Plane face and edge at right angles with try-plane. Gauge thickness and plane down.

2. Proceed as in Model No. IX. 4, making the work first rectangular, then octagonal, and then sixteen sided. Round with try and smoothing-plane (the planing to be done from the lower to the upper end).

3. Measure the length, and saw off at right angles with tenon saw. Shape the ends with knife.

4. Smooth with file and scraper.

Exercises.—*Sawing off, long sawing, face planing, squaring, gauging, long oblique planing, bevel planing, modeling with plane, convex cut, filing, scraping.*

Model No. XXXVII.

Meter Measure of W. B.

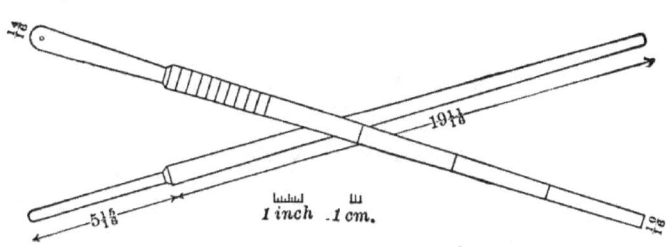

Length, 25⅛ in., or 65 cm. Breadth, ⅞ in., or 2.2 cm.

1. Prepare wood as in previous exercises. Plane face and edge at right angles. Gauge breadth and thickness, and plane down.

2. Lay out on each end the finished width, and connect these points by lines indicating the taper. Plane down to these lines with try-plane. Mark out the divisions with compass, try-square, and brad-awl.

3. Measure the length, and saw off at right angles with tenon saw.

4. The position of the hole is laid out with compass and bored with center-bit.

5. Outline diagram of handle, and shape with chisel and knife. Smooth with file and scraper.

Exercises.—*Sawing off, long sawing, edge planing,*

squaring, gauging, oblique planing, setting out (marking division lines with chisel), boring with center-bit, cross cut, oblique chiseling, perpendicular chiseling, long cut, convex cut, filing, scraping.

Model No. XXXVIII.

Pen Box of W. B.

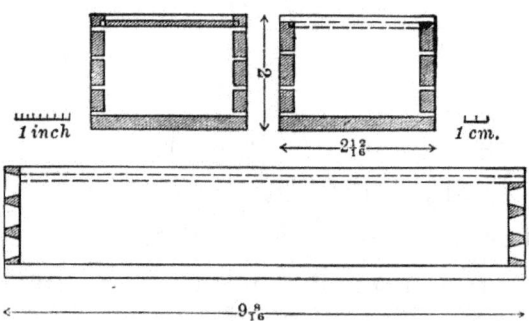

Length, 9 9/16 in., or 24.1 cm.   Breadth, 2 13/16 in., or 7 cm.

1. Regarding the planing of the parts and the dovetailing, refer to Model No. XXXIII.

2. The groove in which the cover slides is made with gauge, knife, and chisel.

3. Fit the cover into the groove with smoothing-plane. The bottom of the box is smoothed with smoothing-plane and glued down. Hold in clamps or hand screws until the glue has hardened.

4. Smooth the outer surfaces with smoothing-plane and scraper.

Exercises.—*Sawing out, long sawing, face planing, edge planing, squaring, gauging, planing in shooting-board, common dovetailing, grooving with knife and chisel, gluing with use of clamps, fixing with wooden pegs (for planing thin wood), cross cut, smoothing up, scraping.*

Model No. XXXIX.

Stool of W. W.

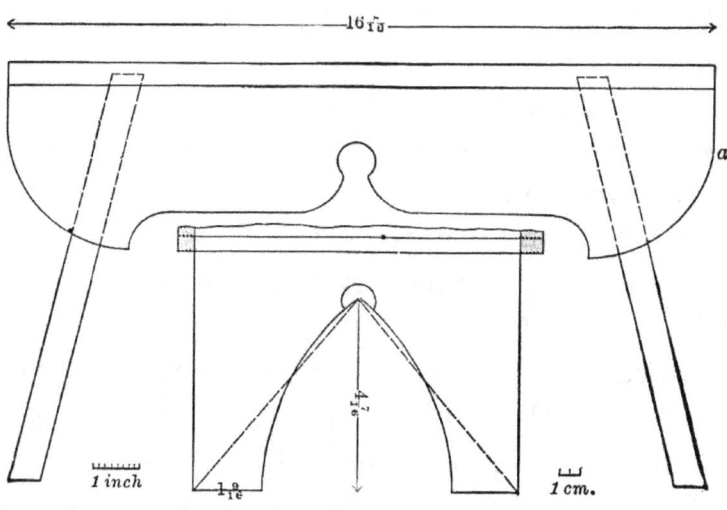

1.

FUNDAMENTAL SERIES 161

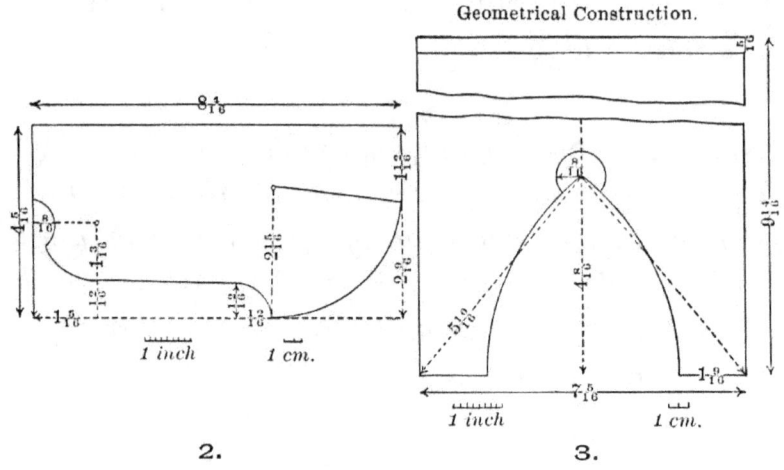

Geometrical Construction.

2. *Length*, $16\frac{8}{16}$ *in.*, *or* 42 *cm.*

3. *Breadth*, $8\frac{4}{16}$ *in.*, *or* 21 *cm.*

1. Saw out the parts as in previous exercises. Plane face and edge of each at right angles. Measure breadth of each and plane down. Gauge thickness of each and plane down.

2. Nail together with two nails the parts intended for the legs so that both legs may be made at the same time.

3. Measure the length, saw off with cross-cut saw, smooth the upper ends in shooting-board with try-plane.

4. Mark out the angle of inclination of the legs with bevel and marking gauge, and plane down to the line with smoothing-plane.

5. Outline diagram of the legs with try-square and compass, and bring out the form with

center-bit, compass saw, and knife. Smooth with file.

6. Measure the length of the top piece, and saw off at right angles with tenon saw. Smooth the edges with smoothing-plane.

7. Mark out the position of the grooving for the legs with compass, try-square, marking awl, bevel, and marking gauge.

8. Make the grooving with knife, tenon saw, chisel, and rabbet-plane.

9. Draw diagonals on the upper side of the top piece, in order to find its center.

10. Lay out the position of the oval opening in the top piece, and make same with center-bit, keyhole saw, knife, and file (boring two holes with center-bit, and sawing between these holes with keyhole saw).

11. After fitting the legs carefully into the groove with knife, glue them into position.

12. Nail together the two pieces intended for the sides.

13. Outline diagram as in geometrical construction (2), and finish to these lines with tenon saw, frame compass saw, smoothing-plane, chisel, knife, and file.

14. Nail down the side pieces. Drive the nails below the surface, using the nail-set and hammer.

FUNDAMENTAL SERIES

15. Smooth the top and side surfaces with try-plane and smoothing-plane.

16. Smooth all other surfaces with file and scraper.

Exercises.—*Sawing off, long sawing, face planing, edge planing, plain jointing, squaring, gluing, gauging, end planing, oblique planing, boring with centerbit, convex sawing, convex cut, filing, oblique edge grooving, sawing with keyhole saw, wave sawing, concave cut, long cut, perpendicular chiseling, nailing, oblique cut, bevel cut, punching in nails, smoothing up, scraping.*

Model No. XL.

Try-square of W. B.

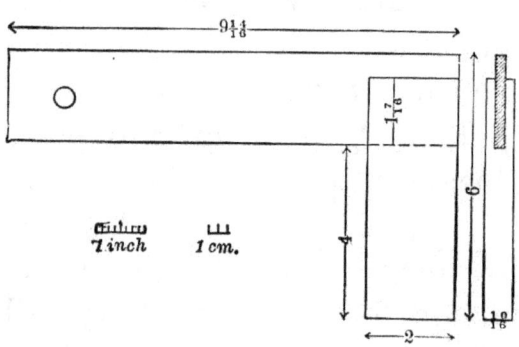

Length, 9 1/4 in., or 25 cm.   Breadth, 2 in., or 5 cm.

1. Saw out the two parts (stock and blade) with rip and cross-cut saw. Plane face and edge

of each at right angles. Gauge breadth and thickness and plane down.

2. Smooth one end of the stock in shooting-board with try-plane. Mark out the position of the open mortise for the blade with compass, try-square, and mortise gauge. Fit the stock and blade carefully together. Glue and hold in clamps or hand screws.

3. Smooth all outer surfaces with smoothing-plane.

4. Measure the length, and saw off at right angles with tenon saw.

5. Smooth the end surfaces in shooting-board with try-plane. Mark out the position of the hole with compass and try-square; bore hole with center-bit.

6. Smooth with scraper.[1]

Exercises.—*Sawing off, long sawing, face planing, edge planing, squaring, gauging, planing in shooting-board, slotting (mortising with saw and chisel), gluing with use of clamps, boring with center-bit, smoothing up, scraping, working in hard wood.*

[1] In making this model, it is of the utmost importance that special care be taken to work down to exact dimensions. It is necessary that the try-square be made absolutely accurate, and therefore no wood should be used which has not been thoroughly seasoned.

Model No. XLI.

Plate Rack of W. W.

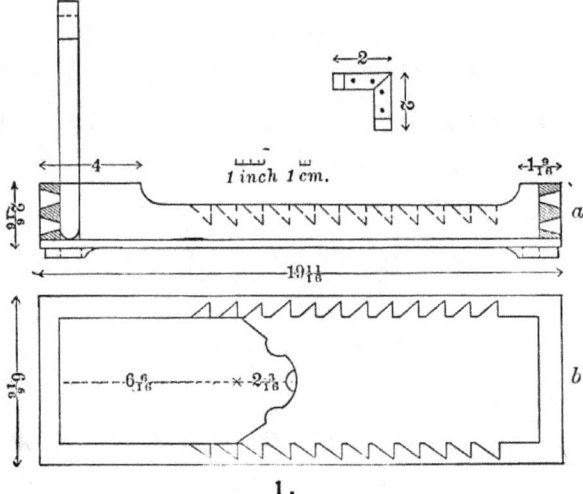

1.

Geometrical Construction.

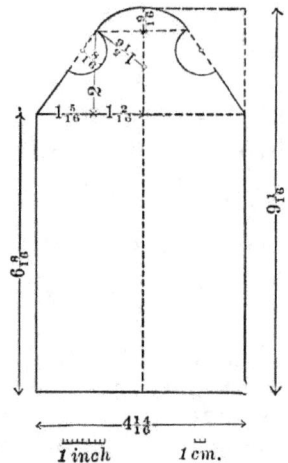

Length, 19 11/16 in., or 50 cm.   **2.**   Breadth, 6 5/16 in., or 16 cm.

1. Saw out the parts for the sides with rip saw.

2. Plane face and edge at right angles with jack and try-plane. Gauge breadth and thickness and plane down. Measure the length, and saw off at right angles with tenon saw. Smooth the ends in shooting-board with try-plane.

3. The dovetailing is made as in Model No. XXXI. Nail the two long sides together. Outline diagram of the form on opposite surfaces with compass, try-square, and gauge. Bring out the form with frame compass saw, gouge, spokeshave, knife, and file. Separate the parts.

4. Mark out the position of the notches with compass, try-square, and gauge, and cut same with tenon saw and knife.

5. Smooth the inner surfaces with smoothing-plane. Glue the parts together.

6. Saw out the piece for the bottom. Plane face and edge at right angles. Measure breadth, gauge thickness, and plane down.

7. Smooth the lower edges of the four sides with smoothing-plane. Nail down the bottom piece.

8. Smooth all the outer surfaces with try-plane and smoothing-plane.

9. Saw out a suitable piece for the four feet. Plane face and edge at right angles. Outline

diagram with try-square and compass, and form with chisel and gouge. Nail down.

10. Saw off a suitable piece for the plate-rest. Plane face and edge at right angles.

11. Measure breadth, gauge thickness, and plane down.

12. Saw off at one end at right angles with tenon saw. Smooth in shooting-board with smoothing-plane. Outline diagram of plate-rest as in geometrical construction (2) with try-square and compass.

13. Form with center-bit, compass saw, smoothing-plane, chisel, gouge, and file.

14. Mark out the position of the two holes in the long sides in which nails are to be driven to hold the plate-rest. (These nails form pivots upon which the plate-rest may be turned down when not in use.)

15. Bore the holes with brad-awl, and nail the plate-rest in place.

16. Smooth the entire model with scraper.

Exercises.—*Sawing off, long sawing, face planing, edge planing, squaring, gauging, planing in shooting-board, dovetailing in thick wood, convex sawing, smoothing with spokeshave, perpendicular gouging, long cut, cross sawing with tenon saw,* *oblique cut, cross cut, smoothing up, gluing, nailing, punching in nails, mitering, oblique chiseling, end planing, boring with center-bit, oblique sawing, oblique planing, perpendicular chiseling, modeling with plane, oblique gouging, boring with brad-awl, fitting axle, scraping.*

Model No. XLII.

Marking Gauge of W. B.

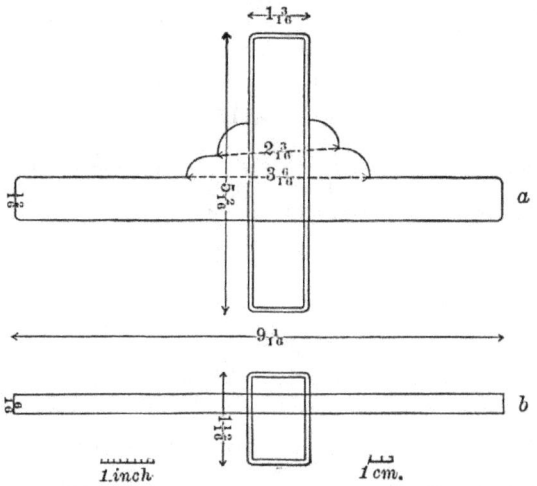

Length, 5 2/16 in., *or* 13 cm.   Breadth, 1 3/4 in., *or* 4.5 cm.

1. Saw out the several parts (head or stock, bar, wedge, and key)[1] with rip and cross-cut saw.

---

[1] The marking gauge consists of four parts. The stock is the handle. The bar is the blade which moves up and down in the stock. The wedge holds the bar in position. The key is a smaller wedge.

Plane face and edge of each at right angles. Gauge the breadth and thickness and plane down.

2. Mark the position of the mortise with compass, try-square, and marking gauge,[1] and make same with firmer-chisel and mallet.

3. Measure the length of the head or stock, and saw off with tenon saw. Shape its ends with chisel.

4. Fit the bar into the mortise with smoothing-plane. Measure the length of the bar, and saw off with tenon saw. Shape with knife.

5. Make the wedge and the key with tenon saw, smoothing-plane, chisel, and knife.

6. Smooth all the parts with file and scraper, and fit together.

Exercises.—*Sawing off, long sawing, face planing, edge planing, squaring, gauging, mortising (common and oblique), perpendicular chiseling, smoothing up, cross cut, long cut, convex cut, modeling with plane, filing, scraping, boring with brad-awl.*

---

[1] In American shops it is customary to place the gauge in the left hand and push it forwards. The Swedes use either hand, and they pull the gauge toward the body, or push it away from it, as happens to be most convenient under the circumstances.

Model No. XLIII.
Rake Head of W. B. and Alder or Ash.

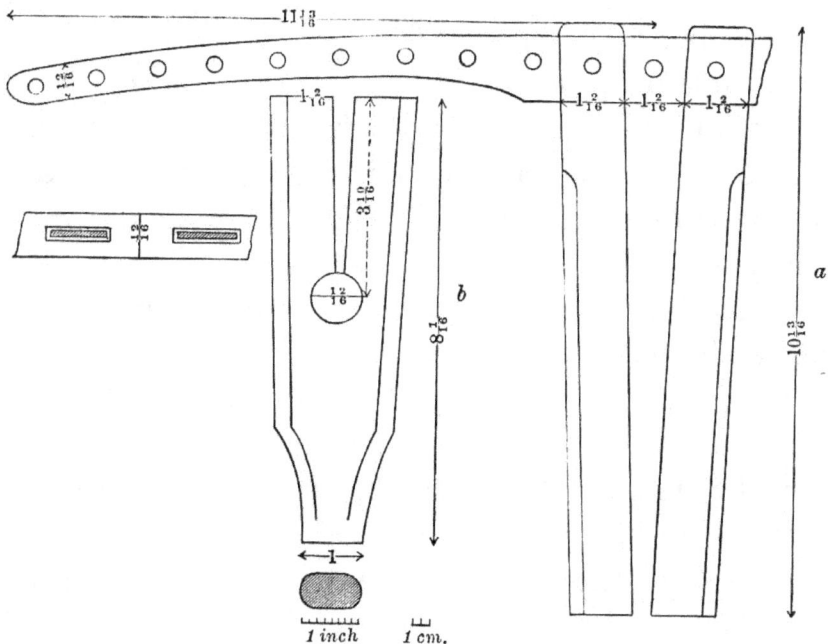

Length, $23\frac{1}{8}$ in., or 60 cm. Breadth, $1\frac{3}{16}$ in., or 3 cm.

1. Saw off a suitable piece for the curved top and plane face and edge at right angles. Outline diagram as in drawing (a).

2. Saw out with frame saw, and finish to the lines with smoothing-plane, spokeshave, chisel, and file.

3. Saw from block a suitable piece of alder or ash for the handle. Plane face and edge at right angles.

4. Outline diagram with try-square and compass, and shape with try-plane, center-bit, rip saw, knife, and file.

5. Taper with jack and try-plane.

6. Outline position of the mortises in the top piece in which the handle is to be fitted with try-square, bevel, and mortise gauge, and make the mortises with firmer-chisel and mallet. Fit the parts together with chisel.

7. Measure the length of the handle, and saw off with tenon saw.

8. Draw a center line on one side of the top piece, and mark out the position of the holes for the teeth with compass. Bore holes with a suitable pin-bit.[1]

9. Gauge the thickness and plane down with try-plane.

10. Smooth entire model with file and scraper.

Exercises.—*Sawing off, convex sawing, face planing, smoothing up, squaring, smoothing with spokeshave, perpendicular chiseling, oblique sawing, oblique planing, boring with center-bit, long cut, gauging, mortising (common and oblique,) bevel cut, concave cut, cross cut, boring with shell-bit, filing, scraping.*

[1] In order to make the openings perfectly smooth, it is best to bore with pin-bit from opposite sides.

Model No. XLIV.

Picture Frame of W. B.

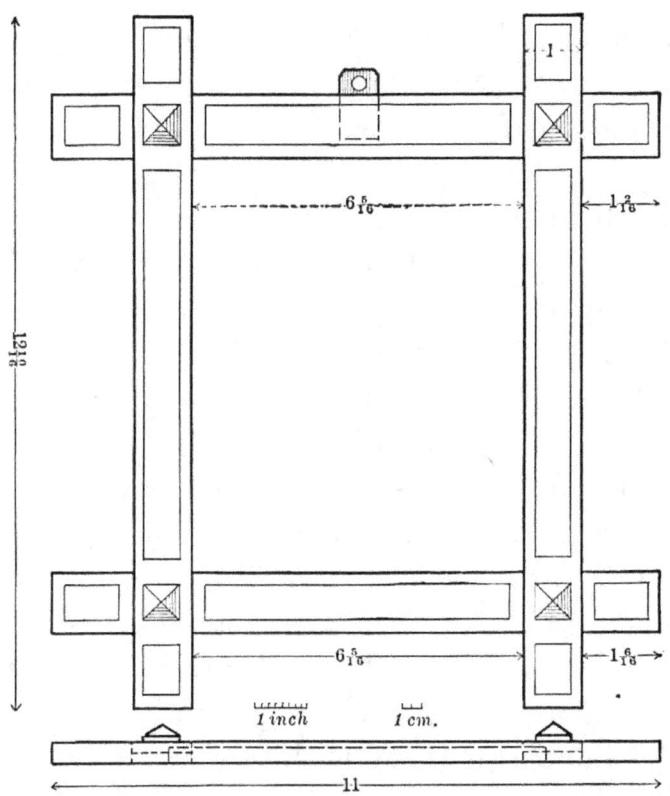

Length, 12¹⁰⁄₁₆ in., or 32 cm.   Breadth, 11 in., or 28 cm.

1. Saw out the several parts with rip and crosscut saw. Plane face and edge of each at right angles. Gauge breadth and thickness and plane down.

2. Measure the length of the pieces intended for the four sides. Saw off at right angles with tenon saw. Smooth the ends in shooting-board with try-plane.

3. Mark out the position of the half-lap joints with try-square, marking awl, and gauge, and make same with tenon saw and chisel (halving with saw and chisel).

4. Fit the parts and glue together.

5. Smooth on outside and inside surfaces with smoothing-plane.

6. The rabbet on the rear side in which the picture back is to be fitted is made with marking gauge, chisel, and knife.

7. Mark out the position of the graving with compass, try-square, and gauge. Make same with V-tool or knife.

8. Make the hanger with smoothing-plane, center-bit, and chisel. Make a groove for same with tenon saw and chisel. Glue in.

9. The small square pyramids which ornament the outer surface of the frame are made in one piece with try-plane. Saw off to required length with tenon saw. Smooth ends in shooting-board and shape with chisel. Glue down.

10. Smooth the ends of the piece intended for the picture back in shooting-board with try-plane.

Fit into the rabbet. Smooth entire model with scraper.

Exercises.—*Sawing off, long sawing, face planing, edge planing, squaring, gauging, planing in shooting-board, halving with saw and chisel, gluing, smoothing up, rabbeting, plain jointing, fixing with wooden pegs, oblique chiseling, graving with V-tool, boring with center-bit, cross sawing with tenon saw, perpendicular chiseling, cross cut, bevel cut, filing, scraping.*

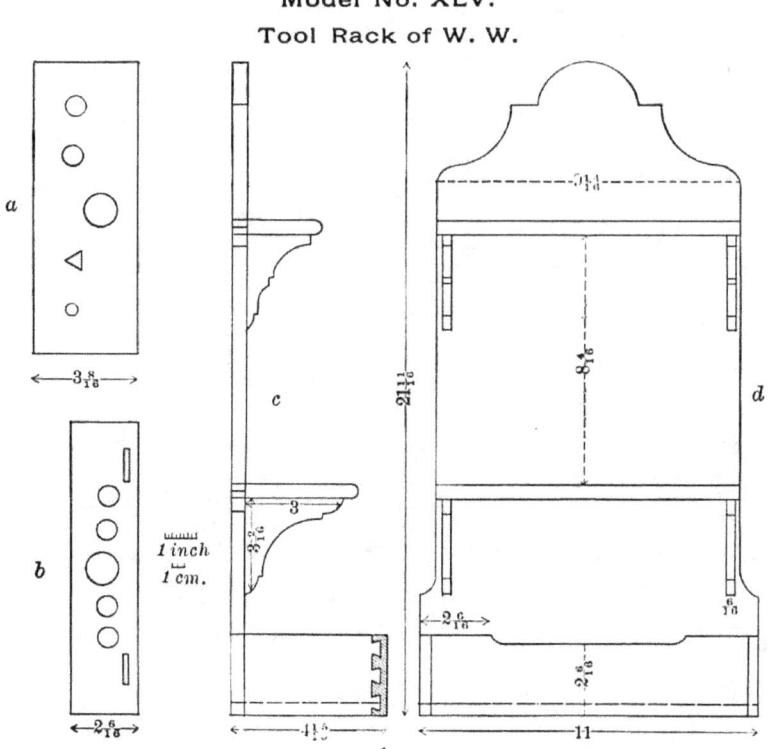

Model No. XLV.
Tool Rack of W. W.

Geometrical Construction.

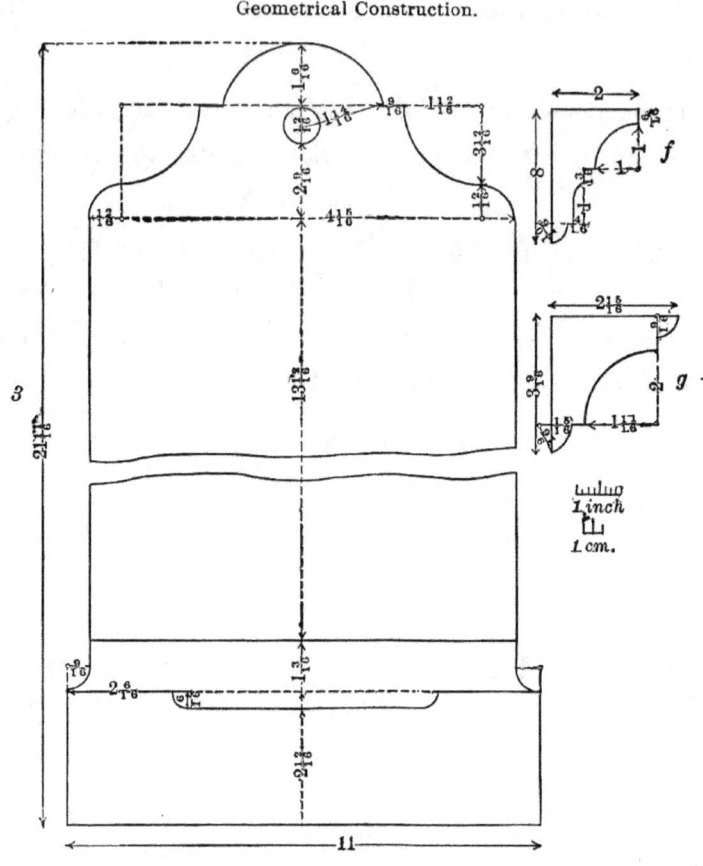

Length, 21⅛ in., or 55 cm.   2.   Breadth, 11 in., or 28 cm.

1. Saw out all the parts with rip and cross-cut saw. Mark off the required breadth, gauge the required thickness of each, and plane down with jack and try-plane. Measure the length of each, and saw off at right angles with tenon saw.

2. The ends of the pieces that are to be dove-

tailed are smoothed in shooting-board with try-plane.

3. Make dovetailing as in Model No. XXXI. (half blind dovetail as indicated by drawing).

4. Outline diagram of the back with try-square, compass, meter measure or rule, and gauge, and finish to the lines with frame compass saw, center-bit, smoothing-plane, knife, and file. Smooth the ends of the bottom in shooting-board.

5. Glue the several parts together.

6. Outline diagram of the front of the box with try-square, compass, and gauge. Bring out the form with compass, knife, and file. Fit together the sides of the box with tenon saw, chisel, and file. Nail down.

7. Smooth all outer surfaces with smoothing-plane. Outline diagram of the brackets—two as in geometrical construction No. 2 (f), two as in geometrical construction No. 2 (g)—and make same with frame compass saw, chisel, knife, and file. Glue these to the back. Nail fast.

8. Plane the ends of the shelves of the brackets in shooting-board.

9. Mark out the position of the holes in the shelves as in drawings 1 (a) and 1 (b) with compass and try-square. Make openings with center-bit and chisel.

10. Provide a suitable piece of sufficient length for the two partitions in the box. Prepare in the usual manner, and glue in position in the box as indicated by the dotted lines of the drawing.

11. Smooth entire model with scraper.

Exercises.—*Sawing off, long sawing, face planing, edge planing, plain jointing, squaring, gluing, gauging, planing in shooting-board, common dovetailing, boring with center-bit, convex sawing, obstacle planing, concave cut, convex cut, cross cut, long cut, filing, half-lap dovetailing, nailing, oblique planing, perpendicular chiseling, modeling with plane, punching nails, smoothing up, scraping.*

Model No. XLVI.

Dough Trough of W. W.

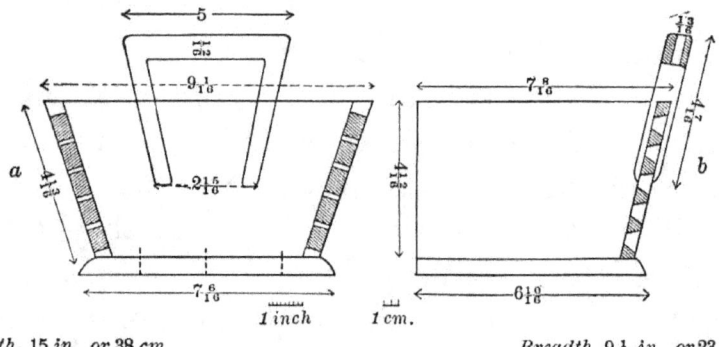

Length, 15 in., or 38 cm.   Breadth, $9\frac{1}{16}$ in., or 23 cm.

1. Saw out all the parts with rip and cross-cut saw. Plane face and edge at right angles with jack

and try-plane. Gauge breadth and thickness and plane down. Measure the length of the four sides with rule, and mark out the angle of the inclination of their ends with bevel and try-square. Saw to the lines with tenon saw. Smooth the ends in shooting-board with smoothing-plane. Smooth the inner surfaces of the four sides with smoothing-plane. Glue the parts together. Smooth the outer surfaces with smoothing-plane.

2. Outline the grooves for the handles to fit in with try-square, bevel, and marking gauge, and make same with knife and chisel. Make each handle in three separate pieces with tenon saw, smoothing-plane, chisel, knife, and file. Fit the three pieces together by means of an open mortise and tenon joint. Glue the two side pieces of each handle in position in the box, then glue the cross pieces fast, and finish the corners with knife and file.

3. Measure the length of the bottom piece. Saw off at right angles with tenon saw. Smooth the ends in shooting-board.

4. Round the edges and ends of the bottom with smoothing-plane and file.

5. Nail down the bottom. Drive nails below the surface with nail-set.

FUNDAMENTAL SERIES

6. Smooth the bottom with smoothing-plane and the entire model with scraper.

Exercises.—*Sawing off, long sawing, face planing, edge planing, squaring, gauging, oblique sawing, oblique planing, double oblique dovetailing, smoothing up, gluing, plain jointing, oblique notching, fixing with wooden pegs, convex cut, long cut, filing, modeling with plane, nailing, punching in nails, scraping.*

Model No. XLVII.

Book Stand of W. W.

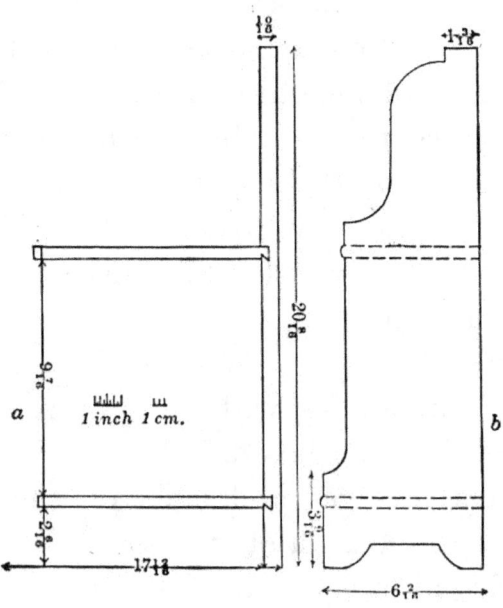

1.

180 NÄÄS MODEL SERIES

Geometrical Construction.

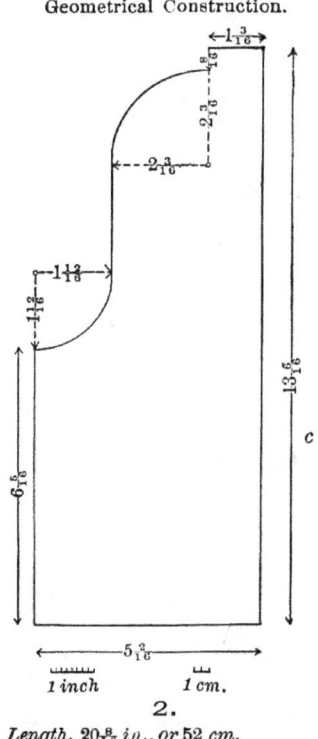

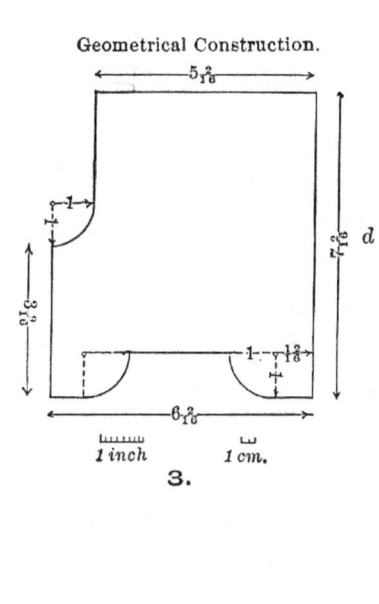

Geometrical Construction.

2.

Length, $20\frac{8}{16}$ in., or 52 cm.   Breadth, $17\frac{12}{16}$ in., or 45 cm.

1. Saw out the several parts with rip and cross-cut saw. Plane face and edge of each at right angles. Measure the breadth, gauge the thickness, and plane down.

2. Nail together the two pieces intended for the sides.

3. Outline diagram on opposite surfaces with try-square, compass, and meter measure. Shape with compass saw, chisel, spokeshave, knife, file, and scraper. Separate the two pieces.

4. The grooves in which the shelves are to be fitted are outlined on the inner surfaces with compass, try-square, bevel, and marking gauge. Make the groove with knife, tenon saw, and chisel. Measure the length of the shelves, and saw off at right angles with tenon saw. Smooth the ends in shooting-board.

5. Round the front edges of the shelves with smoothing-plane.

6. Fit the shelves into the grooves with chisel. Glue fast. Smooth all the surfaces with smoothing-plane, file,[1] and scraper.

Exercises.—*Sawing off, long sawing, face planing, edge planing, squaring, gauging, planing in shooting-board, convex sawing, perpendicular chiseling, smoothing with spokeshave, concave cut, convex cut, cross cut, filing, scraping, half-concealed edge grooving, smoothing up, modeling with plane, gluing.*

---

[1] The proper use of the file in the Sloyd work is very difficult to master. The file should be pushed from the body, never pulled towards it. It is likewise necessary to guard against allowing the file to roll or wabble, as the surface worked upon will become true only when the file is grasped firmly by the handle, and pushed forward with a rapid, steady stroke. It should then be lifted from the wood and placed in its original position. Be careful not to press too heavily upon the wood, as the teeth of the file will then become dull very rapidly. The grooves between the cutting edges should be cleaned from time to time.

Model No. XLVIII.

Hooped Bucket of W. W.

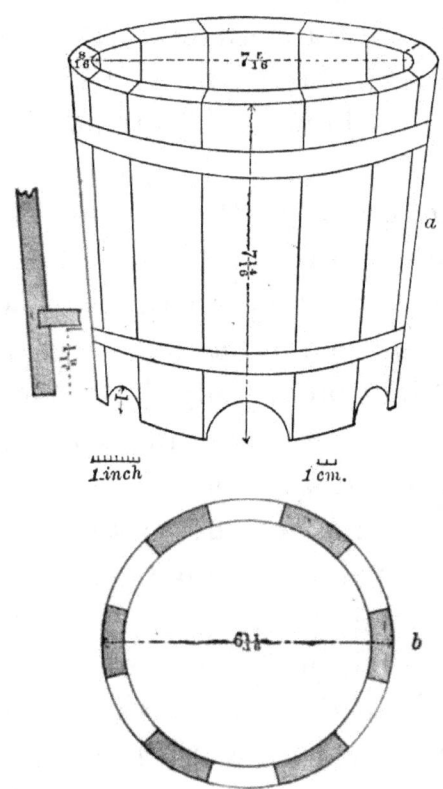

Height, 7⅛ in., or 20 cm.   Diameter, 8¼ in., or 21 cm.

1. Saw out all the parts with rip and cross-cut saw. Plane face, edge, and ends of each stave at right angles with jack and try-plane.

2. Draw on both ends of each stave a curved

line, which is to guide in the planing down, in order to produce the inner concave surface of each stave. Form the concave surface with jack and round-plane.

3. Gauge the thickness of each stave along the edges. Draw on both ends the curved line to guide for making the convex surface. Finish to the lines with hand ax, jack, and smoothing-plane.

4. Outline diagram of the bottom as in drawing 1 (b) with compass. Gauge the thickness and plane down. Bring out the form with frame compass saw and spokeshave.

5. The inclination of edges of the staves is marked out with bevel and marking gauge, and made with smoothing-plane.

6. Outline diagram of the grooves by means of marking awl, bevel, and gauge, on the inner surface of each stave, in which the bottom is afterward to be fitted, making the breadth of the grooves equal to the thickness of the bottom piece. Cut the grooves with knife and chisel.

7. With try-square and gauge mark out the position of the holes in which the little wooden pegs that hold the staves together are to be fitted. Bore the holes with brad-awl.

8. Fit the staves together and set the bottom

into the grooves. Smooth the outer surface of the staves with smoothing-plane.

9. The iron bands which encircle the staves are now made fast.

10. Mark out the required length between the bottom piece and the lower end of the staves by means of the compass. Saw off with tenon saw. Smooth the ends with smoothing-plane and spokeshave.

11. The height is also to be measured from the bottom piece, and sawed off with tenon saw Smooth the upper ends with smoothing-plane and spokeshave.

12. Outline diagram of lower ends as in drawing 1 (*a*), using the compass, and bring out the form with frame compass saw, knife, and file.

13. Smooth the inner surfaces of the entire model with spoon-iron or spoon-gouge, file, and scraper.

Exercises.—*Sawing off, oblique sawing, oblique planing, half-concealed edge grooving, gauging, chopping, modeling with plane, face planing, circular sawing, oblique cut, smoothing with spokeshave, fixing of bucket bottom, boring with brad-awl, hooping, convex sawing, concave cut, bevel cut, end planing, filing, scraping.*

Model No. LXIX.

Cabinet of W. W.

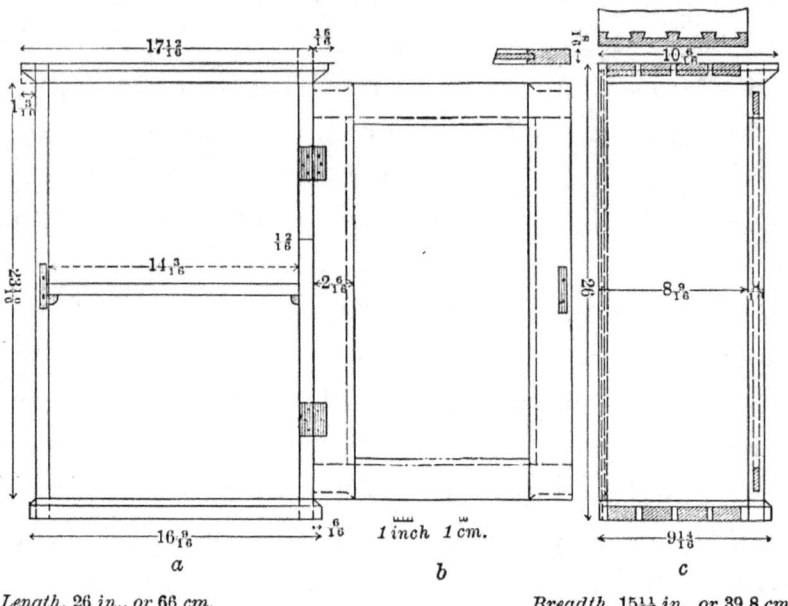

Length, 26 in., or 66 cm.   *Breadth*, 15¼ in., or 39.8 cm.

1. Saw out all the parts with rip and cross-cut saw.

2. Plane face and edge at right angles of the pieces intended for the stiles and rails of the door, and of those for the cornice and base of the cabinet. Gauge breadth and thickness of each of these and plane them down. Outline diagram of the three parts of the cornice and the three of the base, and bring out the form, using jack and try-plane.

3. Plane face and edge at right angles of the pieces for the sides, the top, back, and bottom of the cabinet, and the panel of the door. Measure breadth[1] and gauge thickness of each, and plane down with jack and try-plane.

4. The parts that are to be joined together— viz., the two sides and the top and bottom piece —must be sawed off to their required lengths, and their ends smoothed in shooting-board. The dovetailing is made as in model No. XXXI.

5. Smooth the edges of the two sides with try-plane.

6. The rabbet in the sides in which the back is to be fitted is marked out with marking-gauge and made with knife and chisel.

7. Glue the dovetailing parts together.

8. Saw off the back to its required length and fit it into the groove with smoothing-plane. Nail the back tightly in position.

9. Smooth all the outer surfaces with smoothing-plane.

10. Fit together the parts for the cornice and base with try-square, bevel, and smoothing-plane. Miter them on the corners and nail together.

[1] The breadth of the top and bottom is to be made equal to the breadth of the sides, minus the thickness of the back.

11. The length of the stiles and rails is measured with rule and try-square, and sawed off at right angles with tenon saw. The ends are smoothed in shooting-board.

12. Outline diagram of the through mortise and tenon [1] with relish in the stiles and rails, with try-square and gauge. Make same as in Model No. XLII. with firmer-chisel, tenon saw, and small chisel.

13. Fit the stiles and rails together with chisel. Smooth the outer edges of the stiles and rails with try-plane.

14. The grooves in the stiles and rails in which the panel of the door is to be fitted are laid out with mortise gauge, and made with knife and chisel.

15. Fit the panel of the door into the grooves with try and smoothing-plane. Glue the panel in position. Smooth all surfaces of the door with smoothing-plane.

16. Fix the hinges and lock with try-square, gauge, pin-bit or drill, chisel, knife, brad-awl, and screw-driver.

17. Smooth the top and bottom with smoothing-plane, and the entire model with scraper.

---

[1] Blind mortises and tenons may be used in the construction of the door, as the edges will then present a neater appearance, the ends of the tenons being concealed.

Exercises.—*Sawing off, vertical long sawing (foot-sawing), face planing, plain jointing, gluing, edge-planing, squaring, gauging, end-planing, half-lap dovetailing, grooving with knife and chisel, nailing, beveling with oblique position, mitering, punching nails, smoothing up, mortising, fixing hinges, fixing lock, scraping.*

Model No. L.
Table of W. W.

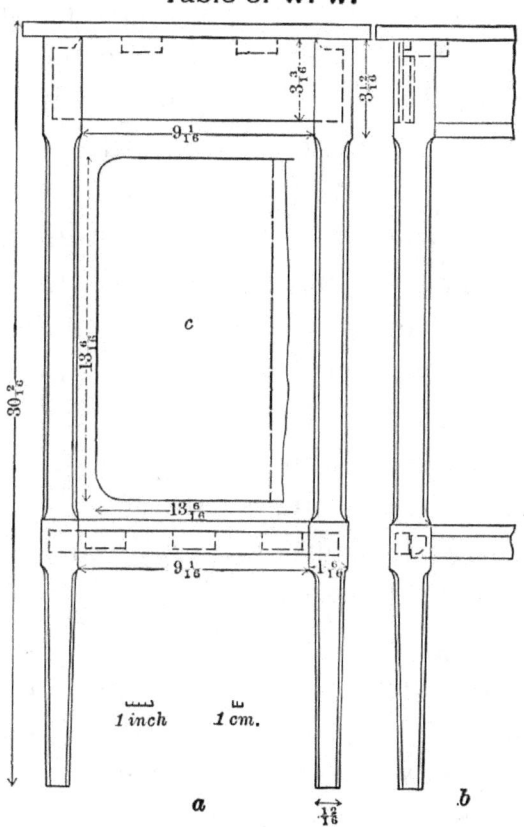

Height, 30 2/16 in., or 76.5 cm.   Breadth, 13 6/16 in., or 34 cm.

1. Saw out the several parts with rip and cross-cut saw.

2. Plane the face and edge of each of the four pieces intended for the legs at right angles. Gauge the thickness of each and plane down.

3. Plane the face and edge of each of the four upper side pieces, or upper rails, and of each of the four lower rails at right angles. Gauge breadth and thickness and plane down.

4. Lay out the tenons as indicated in drawing (*a*) for the blind mortise-joints with try-square and gauge. Make the tenons with tenon saw and chisel.

5. Screw the four legs into the vise of the bench. Lay out the position of the mortises as in drawing (*a*) with try-square and gauge, and make same with firmer-chisel and mallet. Measure the length of the legs and saw off.

6. Construct outline of the legs as in drawing with try-square, compass, and gauge. Bring out the form with jack and try-plane, making the bevel or chamfer with chisel and file.

7. Fit the tenons of the rails into the mortises of the legs, making a blind mortise-joint, with chisel.

8. The grooves in which the eight small mortise blocks that strengthen the table-top are to be

fitted, are marked out on the inside of the four upper rails with compass, try-square, and gauge, and are made with chisel.

9. Glue the rails and legs together.

10. Saw off the upper ends of the legs at right angles and at a level with the upper rails. Smooth the upper edges of the upper rails and the upper ends of the legs with smoothing-plane.

11. Smooth all outer surfaces with smoothing-plane.

12. Plane the face and edge of the pieces intended for the table-top and the shelf at right angles. Measure the breadth, gauge the thickness, and plane down.

13. Fit the shelf in position, using the try-square, gauge, tenon saw, and chisel.

14. The blocks that are to strengthen the shelf are planed in one length. Gauge breadth and thickness and plane down. Mark out the length of each with compass, and saw off with tenon saw. Smooth with chisel.

15. The shelf is held fast to the lower rails with clamps or hand-screws, and the twelve small blocks are glued down on the inside.

16. Lay out diagram of the table-top as in drawing (c) with try-square and compass, and make same with chisel, smoothing-plane, and file.

17. Plane face and edge of the eight mortise-blocks that strengthen the table-top at right angles in one length. Measure the length of each with compass, then saw off, and shape with chisel. Fit the mortise blocks into the grooves. The table-top is held fast to the upper rails with clamps or hand screws, and the mortise blocks are glued into the grooves (the glue being placed only upon the upper surface of each block).

18. Smooth the edges of the top and shelf with smoothing-plane and file.

19. Smooth entire model with scraper.

Exercises. — *Sawing off, vertical long sawing (foot sawing), face-planing, squaring, gauging, edge-planing, haunched tenon (concealed mortising), oblique planing, chamfering with chisel, filing, smoothing up, gluing, plain-jointing, gluing with use of clamps, blocking (gluing with blocks), perpendicular chiseling, end planing, mortise blocking, scraping.*

II. TOWN ELEMENTARY SERIES.[1]

Model No. I. (a). Kindergarten Pointer. (*See page* 103.)

Model No. I. (b). Kindergarten Pointer. (*See page* 104.)

[1] Many of the models in the Town Elementary Series are made in the same way as the corresponding models in the

Model No. II.
Parcel Pin of W. B.

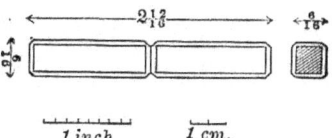

Length, 2⅛ in., or 7 cm.   Thickness, ⅜ in., or 1 cm.

1. A suitable piece of wood is cut four-sided so that it will have the form of a square in cross section.

2. Measure the length and cut off.

3. Chamfer as shown in drawing. Cut the notches. (The entire work is to be done with the knife.)

Exercises.—*Long cut, cross cut, bevel cut.*

Model No. III. Round Flower Stick. (*See page* 105.)

Model No. IV. Penholder. (*See page* 106.)

Model No. V. Rectangular Flower Stick. (*See page* 107.)

Model No. VI. Slate-pencil Holder. (*See page* 108.)

Model No. VII. Key Label. (*See page* 109.)

Model No. VIII. Thread Winder. (*See page* 110.)

Fundamental Series, and many of those in the High School Series are made like those in either the Fundamental or the Town Series. In such cases a reference to the page on which the model has already been described is sufficient.

Model No. IX.

Bar of W. W. (used by the Wood-Carriers).

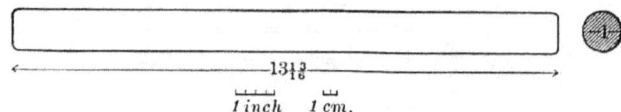

Length, 13⅜ in., or 35 cm.   Diameter, 1 in., or 2.5 cm.

1. Saw from block a suitable piece of wood with rip and cross-cut saws.

2. Plane face and edge at right angles. Gauge breadth and thickness, and plane down with jack and try-planes.

3. Draw diagonals on both ends. With the intersection points as centers, describe circumferences within the squares.

4. Make the object octagonal, then sixteen-sided with try-plane.

5. Round with smoothing-plane.

6. Measure the length and saw off with tenon saw.

7. Round the ends with knife, and smooth entire model with file.

Exercises.—*Sawing off, long sawing, edge planing, squaring, gauging, bevel planing, modeling with plane, convex cut, cross-cut, filing.*

Model No. X.

Pen Rest of W. B.

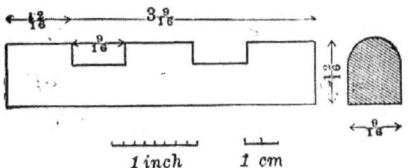

Length, 3 9/16 in., or 9 cm.   Breadth, 13/16 in., or 2 cm.

1. Saw from block as before. Cut to approximate thickness with hand ax.

2. Plane face and edge at right angles. Gauge breadth and thickness and plane down.

3. Measure the length and the position of the recesses with compass. Saw off the length with tenon saw. Cut the recesses with tenon saw and knife.

4. On each end construct a semicircle with a radius equal to half the thickness. Round the upper surface with these semi-circumferences as guiding lines, using smoothing-plane for the purpose. Smooth the ends with knife and the entire model with file.

Exercises.—*Sawing off, chopping, edge planing, squaring, gauging, cross-sawing with tenon saw, long cut, cross cut, modeling with plane, filing.*

Model No. XI. Paper-Cutter. (*See page* 114.)

Model No. XII.

Strop Stick of W. B.

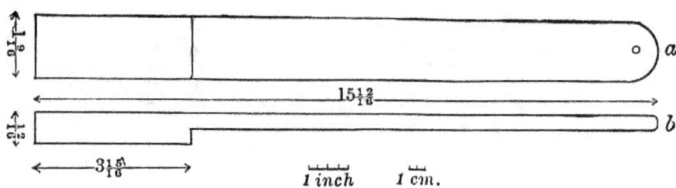

Length, 15¼⅜ in., or 40 cm. Breadth, 1⅜ in., or 4 cm.

1. Saw from block as before.

2. Plane face and edge at right angles. Gauge breadth and thickness and plane down.

3. Construct outline on both edges as in drawing (*b*) with try-square and gauge. Bring out the form with rip saw, smoothing-plane (obstacle planing), and chisel.

4. Saw off the length of the handle with tenon saw. Smooth this end with chisel. Measure the entire length and saw off. Round the upper end with tenon saw and chisel.

5. Bore the hole with center-bit, working from opposite sides. Smooth with file and scraper.

Exercises.—*Sawing off, long sawing, face planing, edge planing, squaring, gauging, obstacle planing, perpendicular chiseling, boring with center-bit, filing, scraping.*

NÄÄS MODEL SERIES

Model No. XIII. Small Bowl. (*See page* 127.)

Model No. XIV. Hammer Handle. (*See page* 119.)

Model No. XV. Spoon. (*See page* 120.)

Model No. XVI. Chopping Board. (*See page* 122.)

Model No. XVII. Flower-pot Cross. (*See page* 123.)

Model No. XVIII.

Meter Measure of W. B.

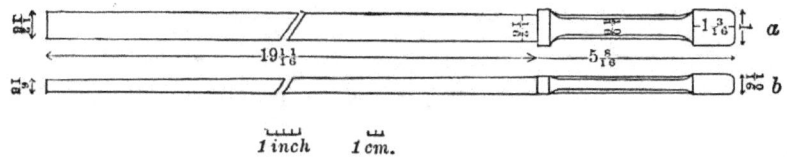

Length, 25⅜ *in., or* 64 *cm.*   *Breadth*, 1 *in., or* 2.5 *cm.*

1. Saw from block a suitable piece of wood as before.

2. Plane face and edge at right angles. Gauge breadth and thickness and plane down.

3. Draw outline of the rule as in drawing (*a*) with try-square and gauge, and make with rip saw, smoothing-plane, and spokeshave.

4. Taper with try-plane.

5. Draw outline of the handle. Saw out with compass saw and shape with knife. Chamfer with knife.

6. Measure length, and saw off at right angles with tenon saw.

7. Smooth entire model with file and scraper.

Model No. XIII. Small Bowl. (*See page* 127.)
Model No. XIV. Hammer Handle. (*See page* 119.)
Model No. XV. Spoon. (*See page* 120.)
Model No. XVI. Chopping Board. (*See page* 122.)
Model No. XVII. Flower-pot Cross. (*See page* 123.)

Model No. XVIII.

Meter Measure of W. B.

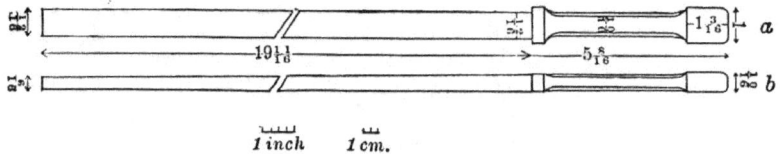

Length, 25 3/8 in., or 64 cm.   Breadth, 1 in., or 2.5 cm.

1. Saw from block a suitable piece of wood as before.

2. Plane face and edge at right angles. Gauge breadth and thickness and plane down.

3. Draw outline of the rule as in drawing (*a*) with try-square and gauge, and make with rip saw, smoothing-plane, and spokeshave.

4. Taper with try-plane.

5. Draw outline of the handle. Saw out with compass saw and shape with knife. Chamfer with knife.

6. Measure length, and saw off at right angles with tenon saw.

7. Smooth entire model with file and scraper.

Exercises.—*Sawing off, long sawing, face planing, edge planing, squaring, gauging, obstacle planing, smoothing with spokeshave, convex sawing, concave cut, long cut, convex cut, cross cut, bevel cut, filing, scraping.*

Model No. XIX. Scoop. (*See page* 125.)
Model No. XX. Clothes Rack. (*See page* 127.)
Model No. XXI. Flower-pot Stand. (*See page* 129.)
Model No. XXII. Ax Handle. (*See page* 131.)
Model No. XXIII. Footstool. (*See page* 132.)

Model No. XXIV.

Book Carrier of W. W. and W. B.

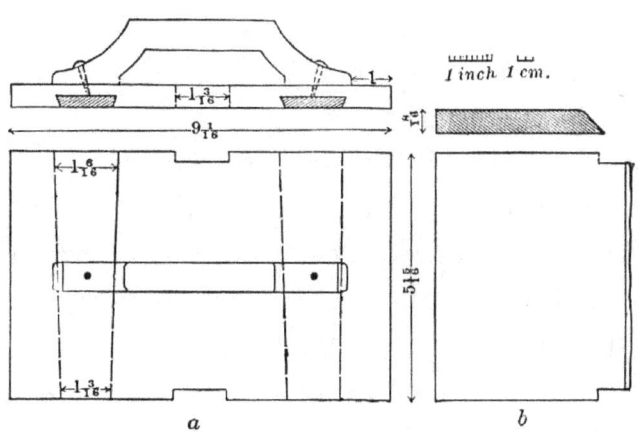

1.

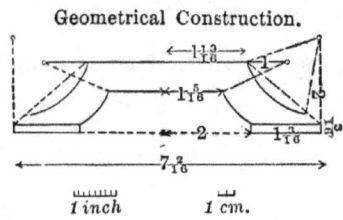

Geometrical Construction.

Length, 9 1/8 in., or 23 cm. **2.** Breadth, 5 1/8 in., or 15 cm.

1. Saw out the two pieces that form the carrier as before. Plane face and edge of each at right angles. Measure the breadth and plane down.

2. Mark out the position of the grooving in the top piece with try-square, compass, meter measure, marking-awl, bevel, and gauge. Cut the groove with tenon saw, chisel, and rabbet plane.

3. Make the two dovetail tongues with jack and try-plane. Fit them into the grooves. Gauge the thickness and plane down.

4. Measure the required length of the parts, and saw off with tenon saw.

5. Nail the parts together. Smooth the ends at right angles with smoothing-plane. Mark out the position of the recesses with try-square and compass, and make them with tenon saw, chisel, and knife. Separate the parts.

6. Saw out a suitable piece for the handle. Gauge breadth and thickness and plane down. Draw outline as in geometrical construction (2)

with try-square and compass, and bring out the form with compass saw, chisel, smoothing-plane, knife, file, and scraper.

7. Bore the holes with pin-bit or drill. Fasten the handle with wood-screws, driving the screws in at a slight inclination.

Exercises.— *Sawing off, face planing, edge planing, squaring, dovetail clamping, beveling with oblique position, gauging, end planing, cross sawing with tenon saw, perpendicular chiseling, long cut, convex sawing, concave chiseling, cross cut, modeling with plane, fixing with screws, filing, bevel cut, scraping, boring with shell-bit.*

Model No. XXV. Box. (*See page* 137.)
Model No. XXVI. Ladle. (*See page* 139.)
Model No. XXVII. Baker's Shovel. (*See page* 141.)
Model No. XXVIII. Clothes-Beater. (*See page* 142.)
Model No. XXIX. Ruler. (*See page* 143.)
Model No. XXX. Bootjack. (*See page* 145.)
Model No. XXXI. Lamp Bracket. (*See page* 147.)
Model No. XXXII. Weaving Shuttle. (*See page* 150.)
Model No. XXXIII. Knife Box. (*See page* 151.)
Model No. XXXIV. American Ax Handle. (*See page* 154.)
Model No. XXXV. Match Box. (*See page* 155.)
Model No. XXXVI. Baseball Bat. (*See page* 157.)

Model No. XXXVII.

Triangle of W. B.

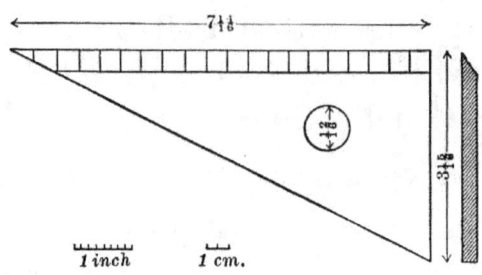

Length, 7 1/8 in., or 20 cm. Breadth, 3 1/8 in., or 10 cm.

1. Saw from block a suitable piece of wood, as in previous exercises.

2. Plane face and edge at right angles with try-plane. Gauge the thickness and saw off with rip saw.

3. Plane to required thickness as in Model No. XXIX., page 144, adjusting the wood upon a foundation piece.

4. Chamfer with try-plane.

5. Smooth the one end in shooting-board with try-plane.

6. Lay out diagram as in drawing with meter measure, try-square, marking awl, and bring out the form with tenon saw and smoothing-plane.

7. Divisions are laid out with the aid of compass, and scratched on the chamfer with try-square and marking awl. Smooth with scraper.

Exercises.—*Sawing off, long sawing, face planing, edge planing, squaring, gauging, fixing with wooden pegs (for planing thin wood), planing with compass plane, beveling with oblique position, planing in shooting-board, boring with center-bit, oblique sawing, oblique planing, setting out, scraping.*

Model No. XXXVIII. Pen Box. *(See page 159.)*
Model No. XXXIX. Stool. *(See page 160.)*
Model No. XL. Try-square. *(See page 163.)*
Model No. XLI. Plate Rack. *(See page 165.)*
Model No. XLII. Marking Gauge. *(See page 168.)*
Model No. XLIII. Rake Head. *(See page 170.)*
Model No. XLIV. Picture Frame. *(See page 172.)*
Model No. XLV. Tool Rack. *(See page 174.)*
Model No. XLVI. Dough Trough. *(See page 177.)*
Model No. XLVII. Book Stand. *(See page 179.)*
Model No. XLVIII. Hooped Bucket. *(See page 182.)*
Model No. XLIX. Cabinet. *(See page 185.)*
Model No. L. Table. *(See page 188.)*

III. HIGH SCHOOL SERIES.

Model No. I. (a). Kindergarten Pointer. *(See page 103.)*
Model No. I. (b). Kindergarten Pointer. *(See page 104.)*
Model No. II. Parcel Pin. *(See page 192.)*
Model No. III. Round Flower Stick. *(See page 105.)*

Model No. IV.

Letter Opener of W. B.

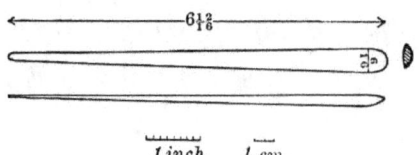

Length, 6⅔ in., or 17.1 cm. *Breadth*, ⅜ in., or 1 cm.

1. Select a suitable piece of wood. Cut to required breadth and thickness.

2. Construct outline as in drawing, and shape with knife, making it first octagonal, then sixteen-sided, and then round.

3. Measure the length and cut off.

4. Round the ends.

Exercises.—*Sawing off, long cut, cross cut, convex cut.*

Model No. V. Rectangular Flower Stick. (*See page* 107.)

Model No. VI. Charcoal and Pencil Holder of W. W. (*See page* 108.)

Model No. VII. Key Label. (*See page* 109.)

Model No. VIII. Pack-thread Winder. (*See page* 110.)

Model No. IX. Bar. (*See page* 193.)

Model No. X. Pen Rest. (*See page* 194.)

Model No. XI. Paper-cutter. (*See page* **114**.)
Model No. XII. Strop Stick. (*See page* **195**.)
Model No. XIII. Small Bowl. (*See page* **117**.)
Model No. XIV. Hammer Handle. (*See page* **119**.)

Model No. XV.

Pen Tray of W. B.

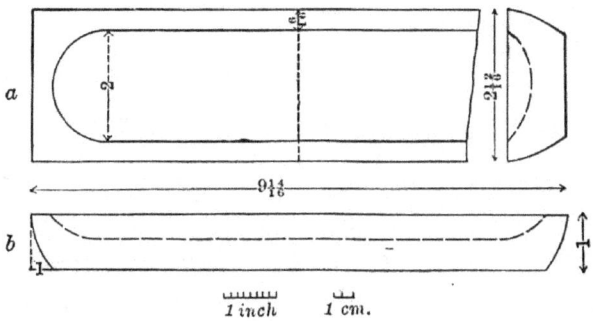

Length, 9 14/16 in., *or* 25 cm.   *Breadth*, 2 3/4 in., *or* 7 cm.

1. Saw off from block a suitable piece of wood. Plane face and edge at right angles. Gauge breadth and plane down.

2. Lay out the position of the hollow as in drawing (*a*) with try-square, compass, meter measure or rule, and gauge. Make the hollow with gouge, mallet, spoon-iron,[1] or spoon-

---

[1] The spoon-iron is rarely, if ever, used in American carpenter shops. It is similar in appearance to our spoon gouge, but it is very much more convenient for deep concave surfaces.

gouge, and smooth with scraper and sand-paper.[1]

3. Gauge the thickness, and plane down with try-plane.

4. Measure the length, and saw off at right angles with tenon saw.

5. Lay out the form of the ends with compass, and shape with chisel and smoothing-plane. Smooth with file.

6. Smooth the outer surfaces of the entire model with smoothing-plane and scraper.

Exercises.—*Sawing off, long sawing, face planing, edge planing, squaring, gauging, gouging with gouge and with spoon-iron, scraping, perpendicular chiseling, filing, modeling with plane, smoothing up.*

    Model No. XVI. Chopping Board. (*See page* 122.)
    Model No. XVII. Flower-pot Cross. (*See page* 123.)
    Model No. XVIII. Meter Measure. (*See page* 196.)
    Model No. XIX. Scoop. (*See page* 125.)
    Model No. XX. Clothes Rack. (*See page* 127.)
    Model No. XXI. Flower-pot Stand. (*See page* 129.)

---

[1] After rubbing this hollow surface with sand-paper, a piece of cork should be used to remove any slight roughness.

Model No. XXII.

Flower-press Roller and Rests of W. B.

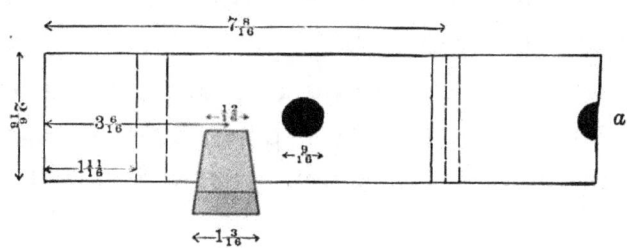

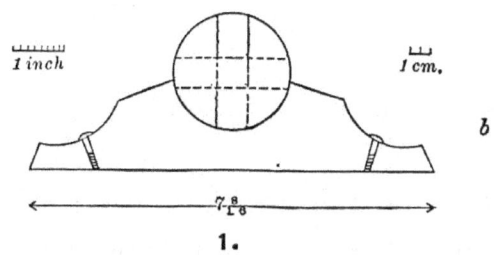

1.

Geometrical Construction.

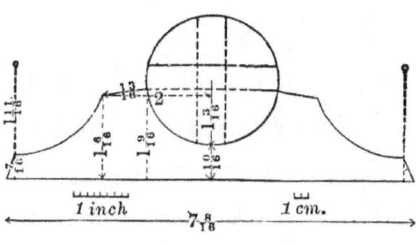

Length, 15 in., or 38 cm. 2. Thickness, $2\frac{8}{16}$ in., or 6 cm.

1. Saw out a suitable piece for the roller. Plane face and edge at right angles. Gauge the

thickness, and plane down with try-plane. Measure the length and saw off at right angles.

2. Lay out the position of the holes with try-square, compass, and gauge. Bore the holes from both sides with center-bit.

3. Construct on each end a circumference within the square. Make the piece first octagonal, then sixteen-sided, and then cylindrical, with jack and try-plane.

4. Smooth with file and scraper.

5. Saw out the pieces for the two rests in one length.

6. Gauge breadth and thickness of each and plane down.

7. Lay out outline as in geometrical construction (2) with try-square and compass.

8. Shape with compass saw, gouge, chisel, and file.

9. The inclination of the upper edges is marked out with compass and meter measure or rule, and is planed down with try-plane. Lay out position of the holes for the screws. Bore them with suitable bit or drill.

10. Smooth the entire model with scraper.

Exercises.—*Sawing off, long sawing, face planing, squaring, gauging, boring with center-bit, bevel plan-*

ing, modeling with plane, perpendicular chiseling, filing, scraping, boring with shell-bit, edge planing, convex sawing, perpendicular gouging, oblique planing.

Model No. XXIII. Footstool. (*See page* 132.)
Model No. XXIV. Book Carrier. (*See page* 197.)
Model No. XXV. Box. (*See page* 137.)
Model No. XXVI. Ladle. (*See page* 139.)

Model No. XXVII.

Flower-press of W. W.

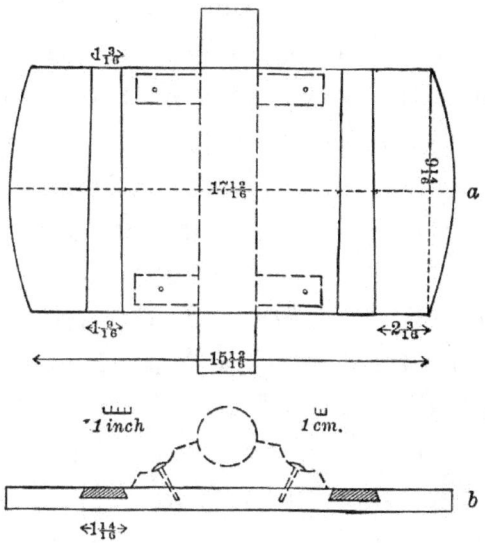

1.

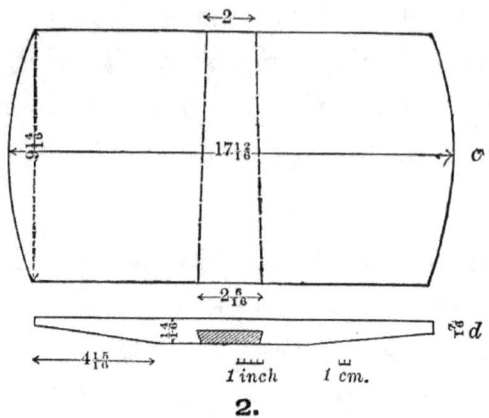

Length, 17⅞ in., or 45.1 cm.   Breadth, 9⅞ in., or 25.1 cm.

1. Saw out the two parts for the top and bottom pieces.

2. Plane face and edge of each at right angles. Measure the breadth of each and plane down.

3. Lay out the position of the grooves by means of compass, try-square, meter measure or rule, marking awl, and bevel. Remove so as to make the grooves with knife, tenon saw, chisel, and rabbet-plane or router-plane.

4. The dovetail tongue is made with jack and try-plane and fitted into the groove.

5. Lay out diagram of the form, and saw out with frame compass saw. Gauge the thickness, and plane down with jack and try-plane.

6. Smooth the ends with spokeshave and file.

7. The inclination of the lower side of the

bottom piece is marked out with compass, try-square, and gauge, and planed down with try-plane and smoothing-plane.

8. Smooth entire model with smoothing-plane and scraper.

Exercises.—*Sawing off, chopping, face planing, plain jointing, gluing, squaring, dovetail clamping, convex sawing, gauging, smoothing with spokeshave, square planing, wedge planing, smoothing up, scraping, modeling with draw-knife.*

Model No. XXVIII.

Coat Stretcher of W. B.

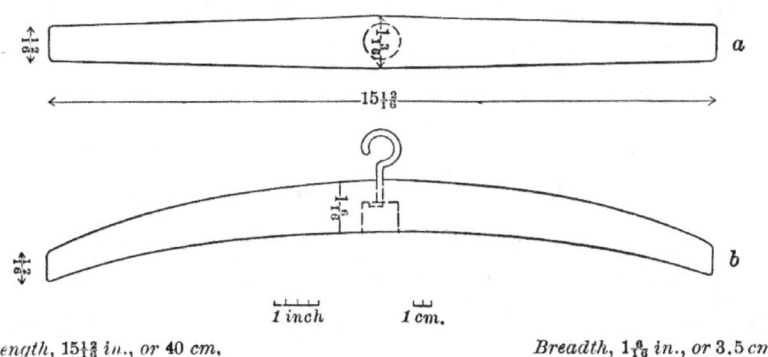

Length, 15⅔ in., or 40 cm.　　　　Breadth, 1⅜ in., or 3.5 cm.

1. Saw out a suitable piece of wood. Plane face and edge at right angles. Gauge thickness and plane down.

2. Lay out outline on opposite edges as in drawing (*b*). Saw out with frame compass saw. Plane down convex surface with smoothing-plane and concave surface with compass or circular plane.

3. Measure the length and saw off. Round the ends with knife.

4. Mark out the position of the holes and bore with center-bit and pin-bit, boring from below with center-bit, and from the top with pin-bit, as indicated in drawing (*b*).

5. Round the edges with spokeshave, and smooth with file and scraper.

6. Fasten the iron hook in position, having previously made a tenon with chisel. Fit this tenon into the hole and glue fast.

7. Smooth entire model with scraper.

Exercises.—*Sawing off, long sawing, face planing, edge planing, squaring, gauging, convex sawing, planing with compass plane, smoothing up, cross cut, convex cut, boring with center-bit, boring with shell-bit, modeling with spokeshave, filing, scraping, sinking iron plates.*

Model No. XXIX. Ruler. (*See page* 143.)
Model No. XXX. Bootjack. (*See page* 145.)

HIGH SCHOOL SERIES 211

Model No. XXXI. Lamp Bracket. (*See page* 147.)
Model No. XXXII. Weaving Shuttle. (*See page* 150.)
Model No. XXXIII. Knife Box. (*See page* 151.)
Model No. XXXIV. Ax Handle (American). (*See page* 154.)
Model No. XXXV. Match Box. (*See page* 155.)
Model No. XXXVI. Baseball Bat. (*See page* 157.)
Model No. XXXVII. Triangle. (*See page* 200.)
Model No. XXXVIII. Pen Box. (*See page* 159.)
Model No. XXXIX. Stool. (*See page* 160.)
Model No. XL. Try-square. (*See page* 163.)

Model No. XLI.
Drawing Board with Frame of W. W.

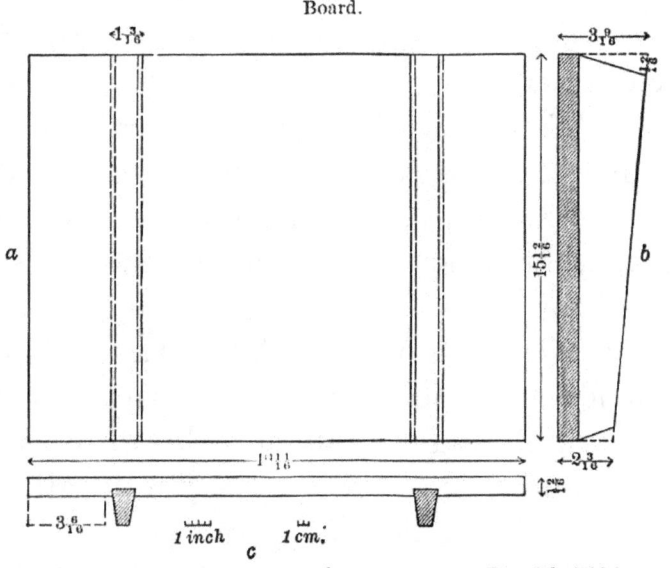

Length, $19\frac{11}{16}$ *in., or* 50 *cm.*   **1.**   *Breadth*, $15\frac{12}{16}$ *in., or* 40 *cm.*

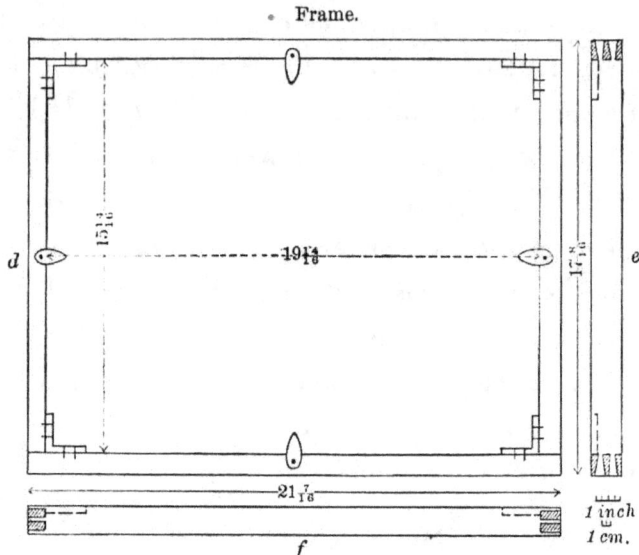

Frame.

Length, 19¼⅛ in., or 50.5 cm.   2.   Breadth, 17⅕ in. or 44.5. cm.

1. Saw out the several parts with rip and cross-cut saws.

2. Plane face and edge of the parts for the frame at right angles. Measure the breadth, gauge the thickness, and plane down. Measure the length and saw off. Smooth the ends in shooting-board.

3. Dovetail as in Model No. XXXIII. (page 152).

4. Plane face and edge of the parts for the board at right angles. Measure breadth, gauge thickness, and plane down. Measure length and saw off at right angles with rip saw.

5. Lay out the position of the grooves with

try-square, compass, meter measure or rule, marking awl, bevel, and gauge. Remove so as to produce the grooves with knife, tenon saw, chisel, and rabbet-plane.

6. The inclination of the sides of the dovetail tongue is laid out with rule and compass, and made with jack and try-plane.

7. Smooth the ends with try-plane and fit into the frame. The small support blocks that strengthen the corners of the frame are planed in one length with try-plane, and sawn off to their required length with tenon saw. Smooth the ends with chisel and nail down.

8. The bolts are planed in one length with try-plane, and shaped with chisel and knife.

9. Bore the holes with brad-awl and screw the bolts down. Smooth entire model with smoothing-plane and scraper.

Exercises.—*Sawing off, long sawing, face planing, edge planing, squaring, gluing, gauging, planing in shooting-board, dovetailing in thick wood, dovetail clamping, end planing, oblique planing, smoothing up, mitering, oblique chiseling, boring with brad-awl, nailing, perpendicular chiseling, long cut, fixing with screws, scraping.*

Model No. XLII. Marking Gauge. (*See page* 168.)

Model No. XLIII.
Bracket of W. B.

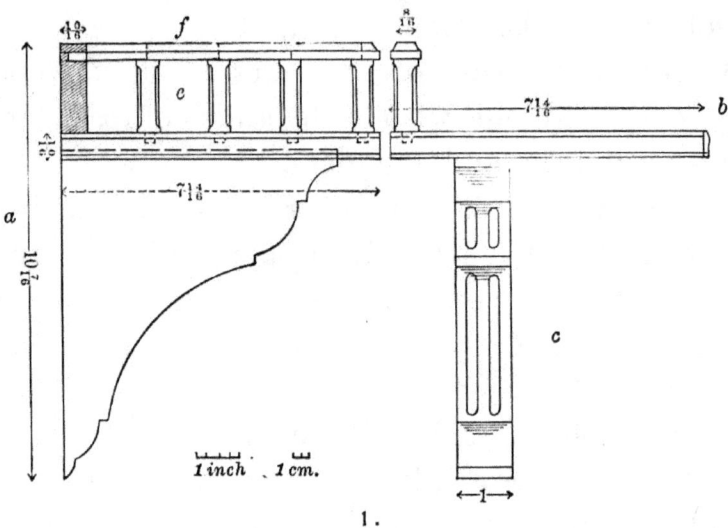

1.

Geometrical Construction.

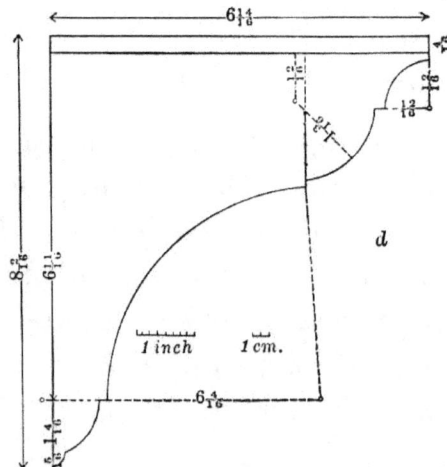

Length, 15⅓ in., or 40 cm.   2.   *Breadth*, 7⅘ in., or 20 cm.

1. Saw out the several parts with rip and crosscut saws.

2. Plane face and edge of the pieces intended for the two bracket supports and the piece for the body of the shelf at right angles. Gauge breadth and thickness and plane down.

3. Nail the parts for the supports together. Draw outlines as in geometrical construction 2 (*d*) with try-square, compass, and meter measure or rule.

4. Saw off the upper end at right angles with rip saw and smooth with smoothing-plane. Bring out the form with compass saw, chisel, gouge, file, and scraper.

5. Lay out the position of the two grooves on the bottom of the body of the shelf, in which the supports are to be fitted with compass, try-square, marking awl, bevel, and gauge. (The depth of the grooves is marked out with mortise gauge.)

6. Remove, producing the grooves with knife, tenon saw, chisel, and rabbet-plane.

7. Saw off the required length of the back and the body of the shelf at the same time with tenon saw.

8. Smooth the ends with smoothing-plane.

9. Glue the supports into position.

10. Smooth the body of the shelf with smoothing-plane.

11. Saw out the pillars (*e*) in one length. Bring out their form with plane, chisel, and knife.

12. The railing (*b*) of the balustrade is made with the try-plane.

13. The distance between the pillars is marked out with compass. The holes in which the tenons of the pillars are to fit are bored with center-bit.

14. Nail the back and body together. Fit the other parts and glue fast. Smooth all outer surfaces with smoothing-plane.

15. The carving on the edges is made with carving-tools.

16. Smooth entire model with scraper.

Exercises.—*Sawing off, long sawing, face planing, edge planing, squaring, plain jointing, gluing, gauging, end planing, convex sawing, perpendicular chiseling, perpendicular gouging, filing, scraping, half concealed edge grooving, smoothing up, concave cut, long cut, bevel cut, mortising, setting out, scraping, sinking iron plates, boring with center-bit, nailing, graving with V-tool.*

Model No. XLIV. Picture Frame. (*See page* 172.)

Model No. XLV. Tool Rack. (*See page* 174.)

Model No. XLVI.

Tea Tray of W. W.

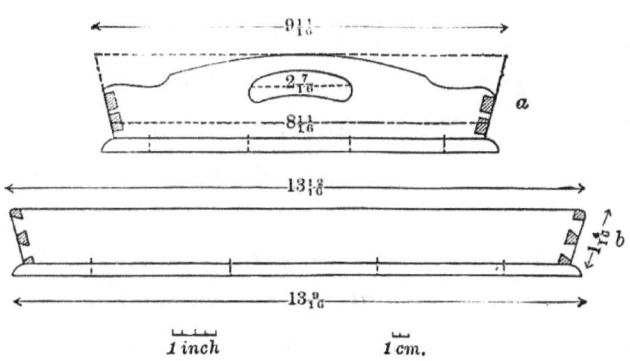

Length, 13⅔ in., *or* 35 cm.   *Breadth*, 9⁷⁄₁₀ in., *or* 24 cm.

1. Saw out the several parts as in previous exercises.

2. Plane face and edge of each at right angles. Gauge thickness, measure breadth, and plane down.

3. Lay off the length of the four sides with meter measure or rule, determining the angles of inclination of the ends by means of level. Saw off with tenon saw and smooth the ends with smoothing-plane.

4. The dovetailing is made as in Model No. XXXIII. (page 152).

5. Draw the outline of the ends and bring out the form with center-bit, chisel, compass saw, file, and knife.

6. Glue the sides and ends together. Smooth the outer surfaces with smoothing-plane.

7. Draw the outline of the bottom and shape with smoothing-plane and file.

8. Nail down the bottom. The upper edges are rounded with smoothing-plane, knife, and file.

9. Smooth the entire model with scraper.

Exercises.—*Sawing off, long sawing, face planing, edge planing, squaring, gauging, plain jointing, gluing, oblique sawing, oblique planing, double oblique dovetailing, boring with center-bit, perpendicular chiseling, convex sawing, long cut, convex cut, concave cut, filing, smoothing up, modeling with plane, boring with brad-awl, nailing, punching in nails, scraping.*

Model No. XLVII. Book Stand. (*See page* 179.)
Model No. XLVIII. Hooped Bucket. (*See page* 182.)
Model No. XLIX. Cabinet. (*See page* 185.)
Model No. L. Table. (*See page* 188.)

CHAPTER V.

EVA RODHE'S MODEL SERIES.

INTRODUCTION.

THE object of all education is to form the character and to strengthen the will power, to develop the intellectual faculties and the ability to work, and to give a healthy physical training. As to this aim, all educators are agreed, as also to the idea that education is the most important factor in the making of the man; but in two other respects there is among educators great difference of opinion: first, as to when the education should begin; and, second, as to what a correct and rational education should comprise.

I believe that the education of the child begins with his consciousness. The foundation for the child's character should be laid in the earliest years of his life. Even at the age of five years, great differences may be noted in the characters of different children, differences which are the result not only of natural or inherited tendencies, but also of the "bringing up." If all parents understood how to educate their children in the right way, without exercising either undue severity or excessive indulgence, if they themselves could serve as worthy examples of what they would have their children be and do, then indeed might we expect our future generations to display a far nobler type of manhood and womanhood. It is the province of the school to assist parents in forming the child's character, to impart information, and to cultivate the power "to do," thereby developing the mental faculties, and last, but not least, to send the child back to the home with a strong and healthy body. In order to accomplish these ends, the school must demand of the pupils that they be truthful, obedient, faithful, diligent, orderly, kind to their comrades, and active and willing in their work. How can this be best accomplished?

As few rules as possible should be laid down for the guidance of the pupil. No pedantry should exist within the class-room, and any tendencies towards it should be discouraged. The lessons should be short and of a character calculated to arouse the interest of the child, so that the work may prove pleasant and not irksome.

When the work is of a healthy character and within the child's capability, then only will the information imparted be of lasting value, and then only can the mind be broadened in all its phases. The course of instruction must not comprise too many subjects to be taught at once. Too many studies tend rather to weaken than to strengthen the mind. In order to develop the physical powers, book studies and practical work must be combined in all the school exercises. If the child spends seven hours a day at school, at least two of these seven hours should be devoted to physical work.

The objections to the present system of education are as follows: first, the children take up the study of abstract subjects at too early an age; second, the subjects succeed one another too rapidly, so that the thorough mastery of any one subject becomes impossible; third, the children are compelled to remain seated and inactive for too great a period of time; and, fourth, they have no practical work.

Up to the age of seven years the child should be busied with nothing but manual work and games, after which theoretical work and practical exercises, manual work, games, and gymnastics should be combined in such a way that one exercise will relieve another, and prevent the child from growing tired.

The books in use must be brief, and some reading-book should be used in every class. The greater part of the time should be devoted to the art of reading, writing, and speaking the mother tongue. Courses in moral instruction, the rules for health, and the laws and customs of the country should be obligatory in every school.

Girls at the age of thirteen or fourteen should receive instruction in matters pertaining to the home, and boys of the same age should be taught the various kinds of manual work.

Froebel's system may be applied to children up to the fifth year. From the fifth to the eighth year suitable manual work should be provided, with the use of light tools; from the eighth to the eleventh year, manual work with larger and heavier tools, in various kinds of wood suitable for the making of simple models; and from the eleventh to the thirteenth year, the Sloyd System of Nääs will be found very valuable.

Eva Rodhe.

Gothenburg, *February*, 1891.

THE EVA RODHE MODEL SERIES.

(A Series for Children from five to eight years of age.)

List of the Models.

All the models are to be made of thin birch or cedar wood; the thickness to be about one fourth of an inch.

I. Fish-line winder.*
II. Key label.*
III. Sewing stand.*
IV. Thread paper.*
V. Palette (play toy).*
VI. Cutting board.*
VII. Darning-needle.*
VIII. Bottle label.*
IX. Clothes hanger (play toy).*
X. Plant label.*
XI. Stocking board (play toy).*
XII. Chopping board (play toy).*
XIII. Potter's knife (play toy).*
XIV. Shovel (play toy).*
XV. Leaf.*
XVI. Flower stick.*
XVII. Butter knife (play toy).*
XVIII. Baker's shovel (play toy).*
XIX. Glass stand.*
XX. Clothes-pin.*
XXI. Pointer.*
XXII. Ribbon holder.*
XXIII. Picture frame (play toy).*
XXIV. Flower-pot foot.*
XXV. Flower-pot spade.*
XXVI. Flower-pot hoe.*
XXVII. Paper-cutter.*
XXVIII. Penholder.*
XXIX. Ladder.
XXX. Lace winder (used in knitting).*
XXXI. Leaf.*
XXXII. Bean-sling (play toy).*
XXXIII. Crochet-needle.
XXXIV. Knife-holder.
XXXV. Bread-board in form of a fish (play toy).*
XXXVI. Soldier (play toy).
XXXVII. Castanets.*

* Drawings of the starred models will be found on pp. 227–234.

XXXVIII. Jack in the box.*
XXXIX. Stand.*
XL. Egg-cup.
XLI. Toothbrush holder.
XLII. Ironing board.
XLIII. Desk protector.
XLIV. Frame saw (play toy).
XLV. Key-rack.
XLVI. Crocodile (letter opener), (play toy).
XLVII. Sledge (play toy).
XLVIII. Easel.*
XLIX. Roller-stand.*
L. Horse and rider (play toy).

THE EVA RODHE MODELS.

Models Nos. II. and XXVII. furnish an illustration of the method of making all of the models of this series.

Model No. II.

Key Label of thin Birch or Cedar.

A piece of wood somewhat larger than the model is placed in the vise of the bench. By means of a spokeshave its rough sides[1] are planed down, and they are smoothed with a scraper. The teacher should draw a straight line close to one of the edges with rule. The child is to saw off close to this line. The edge is now to be smoothed with file. With try-square draw a

---

[1] Here, as in the "Nääs Series," the expression "sides" refers to the two broad surfaces; "edges," to the two narrow surfaces; "ends," to the two in which are the extremities of the fibers.

line close to one of the ends, straight across one of the sides. Saw out and file down to this second line. Lay off 7 cm., or $2\frac{12}{16}$ in., along the edge, and draw a line across one of the sides. With compass lay off a distance of 2 cm., or $1\frac{3}{16}$ in., and describe a semicircle. Saw out and file down. The hole is bored with brad-awl. Smooth with scraper and sand-paper.

Model No. XXVII.

Paper-cutter of thin Birch or Cedar.

Plane down with spokeshave as in previous model. A drawing of the model is made with pencil, rule, and try-square. Saw close to the lines and file down. The cutting edge of the model is made with spokeshave, file, and scraper, working first on one side, and then on the other. The teacher should mark on the object how much is to be worked away. Smooth the model with sand-paper.

Experience has taught us that children of five to nine years of age should not be permitted to use the knife, as they are apt to cut themselves. The tools used in the Eva Rodhe Series are the saw, file, hammer, bit, spokeshave, scraper, brad-awl, marking awl, compass, meter measure or rule, and try-square.

It is best to allow the child to use the saw for a few lessons before he begins the making of the models. Very little sand-paper should be used, and that only where it is absolutely necessary.

The tools are somewhat smaller than ordinary mechanics' tools, being made of such a size and weight as not to overtax the strength of the child.

THE EVA RODHE MODELS

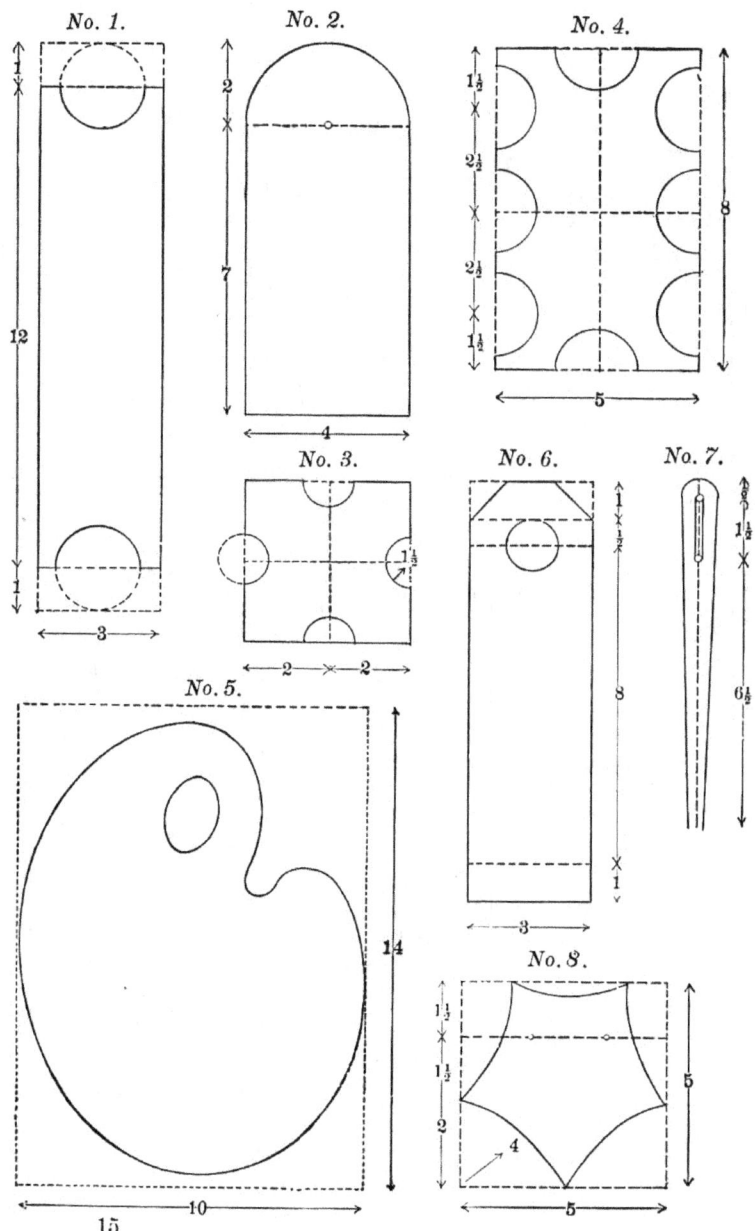

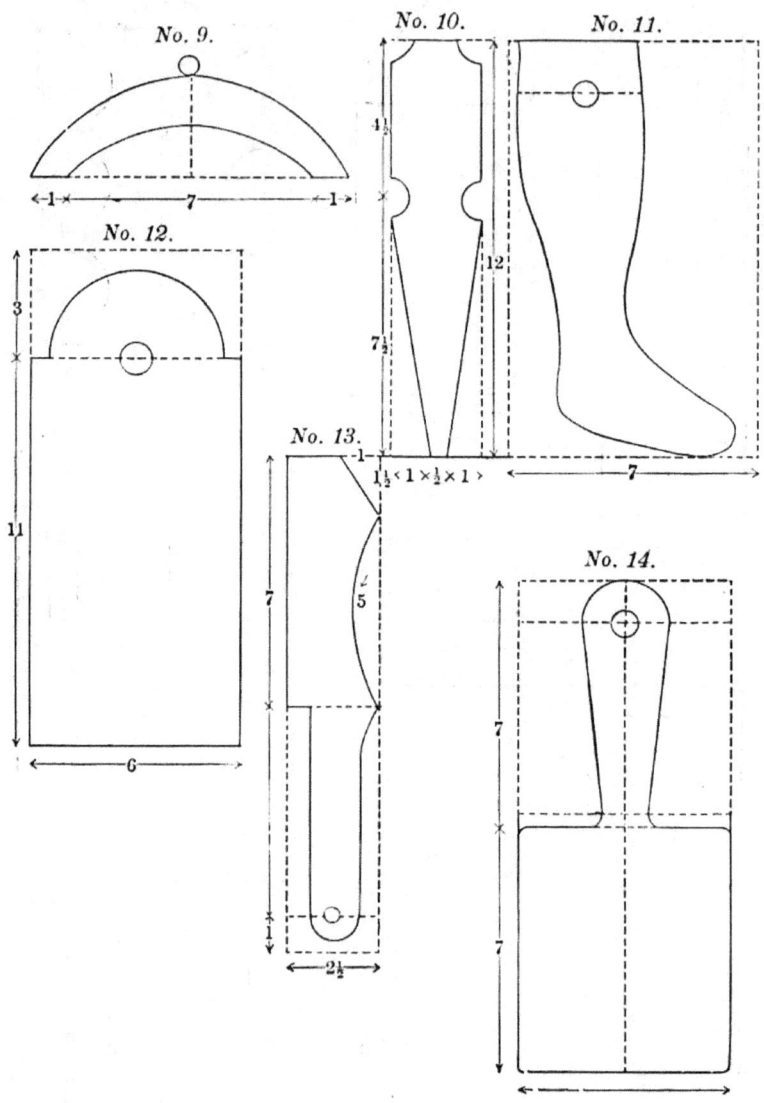

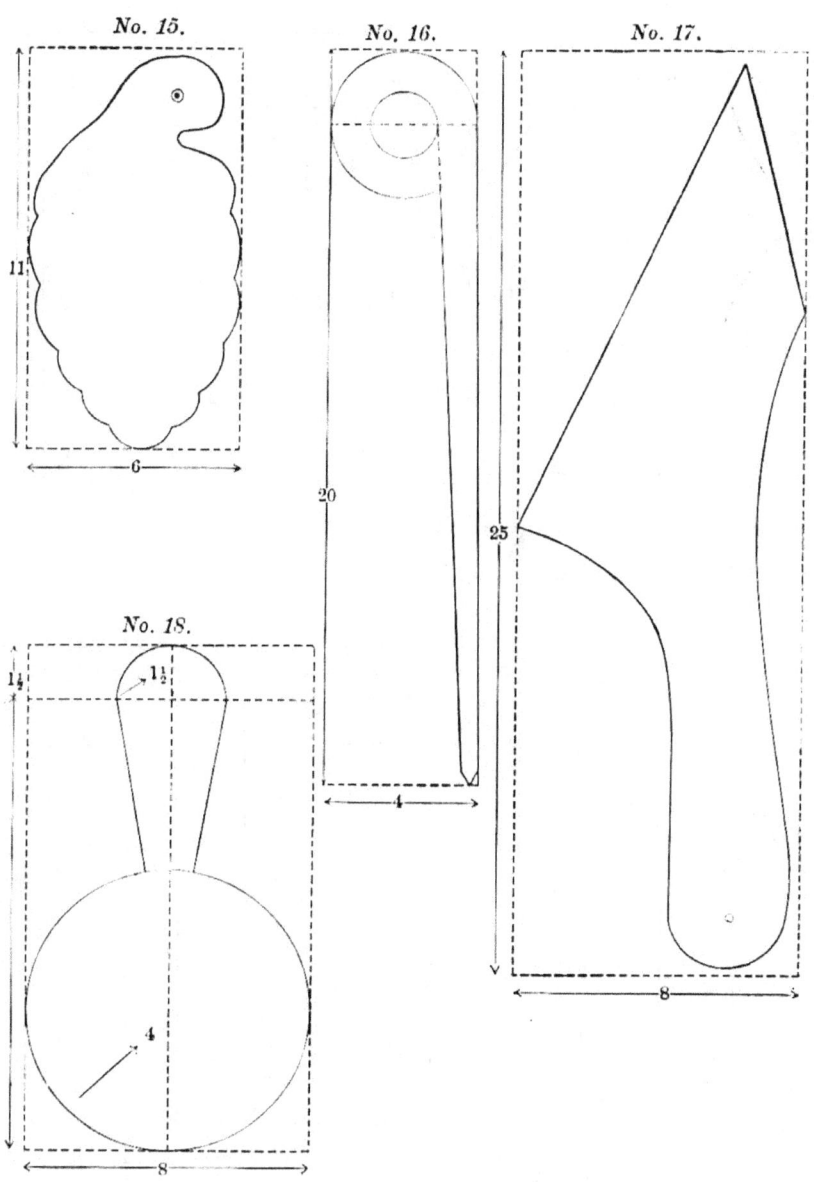

230   EVA RODHE'S MODEL SERIES

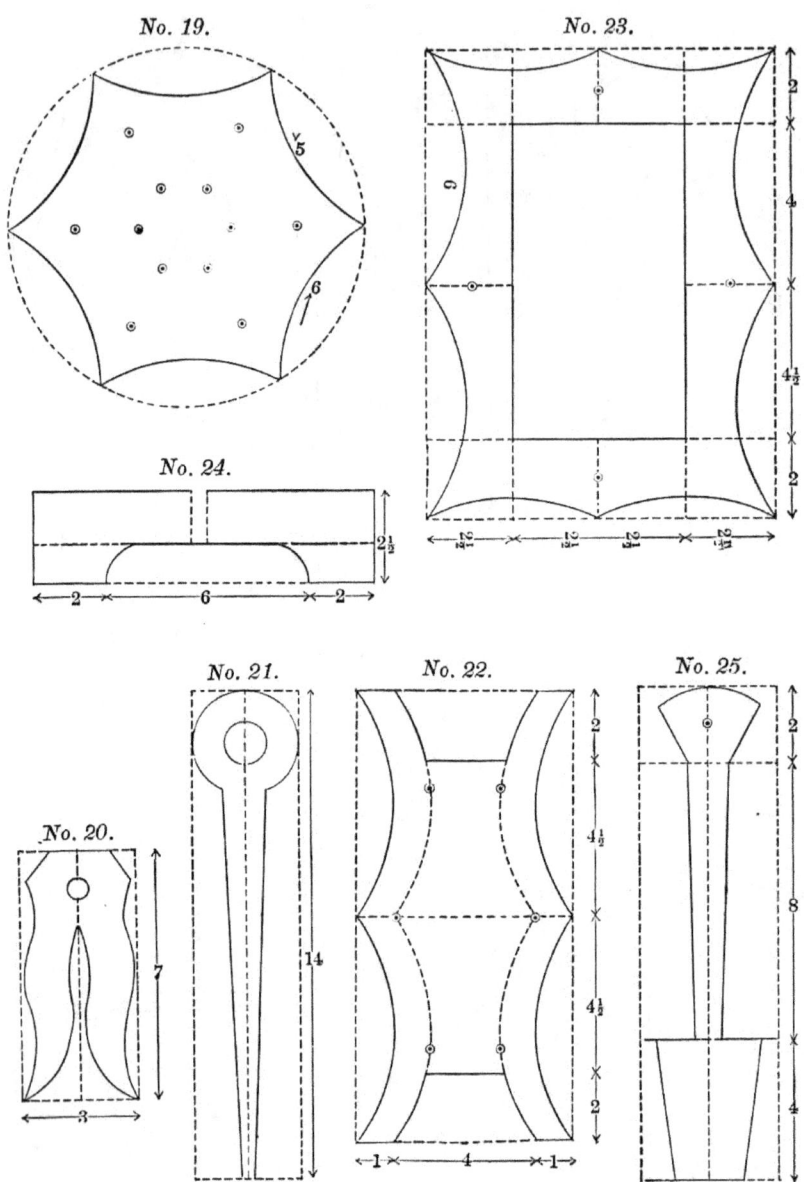

THE EVA RODHE MODELS

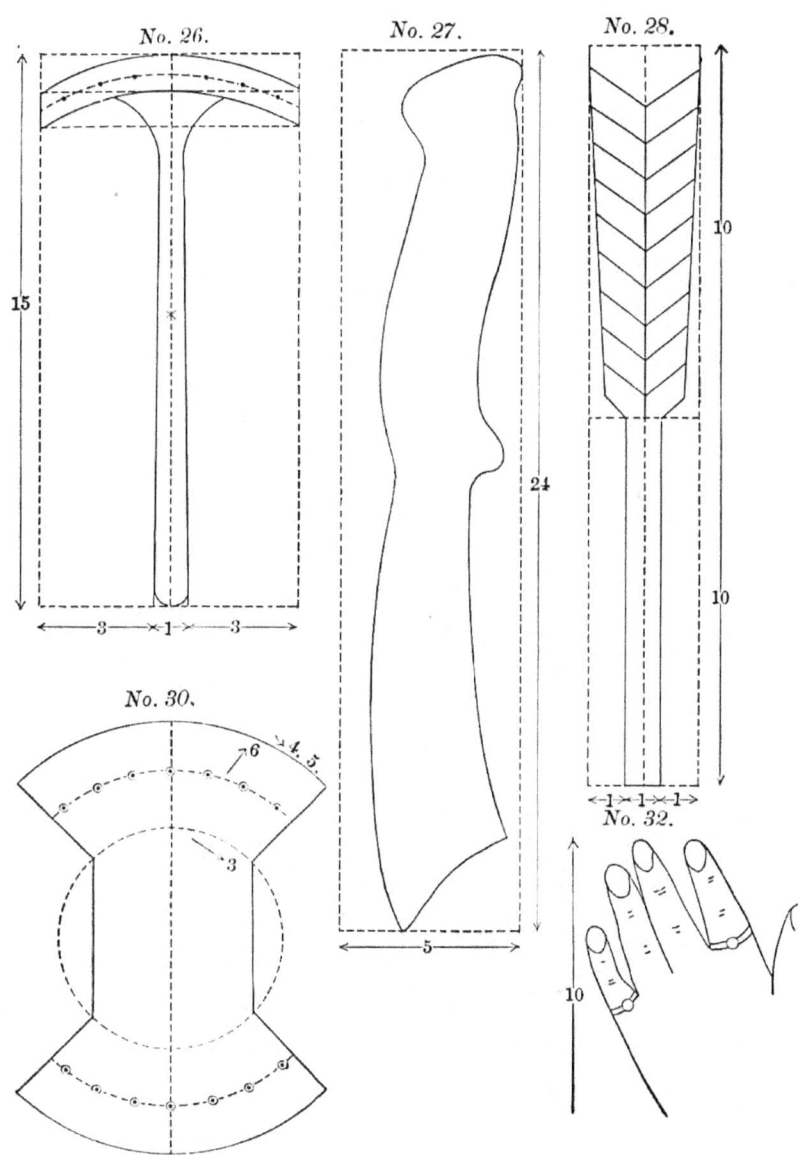

232   EVA RODHE'S MODEL SERIES

No. 31.

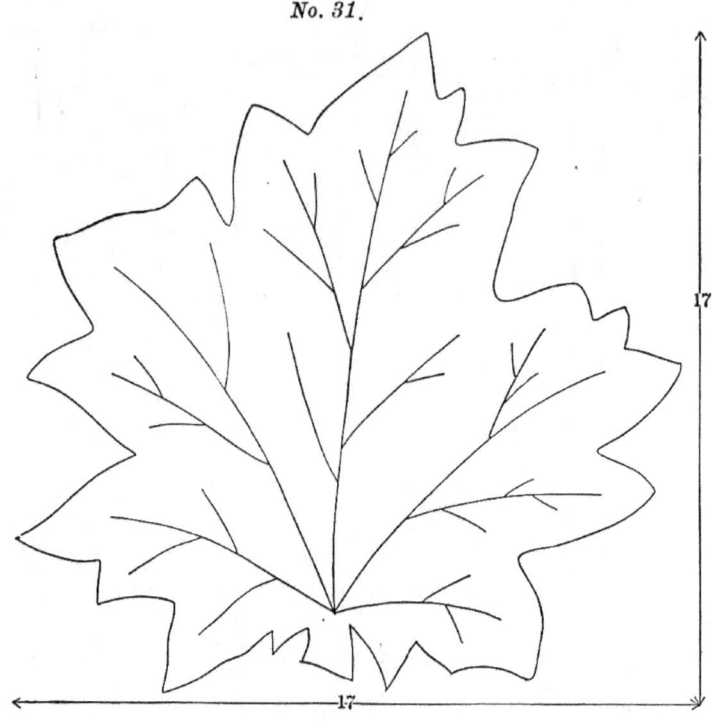

No. 37.

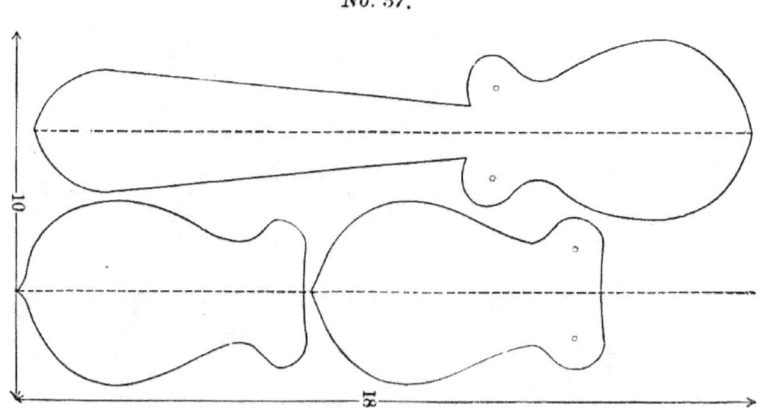

THE EVA RODHE MODELS

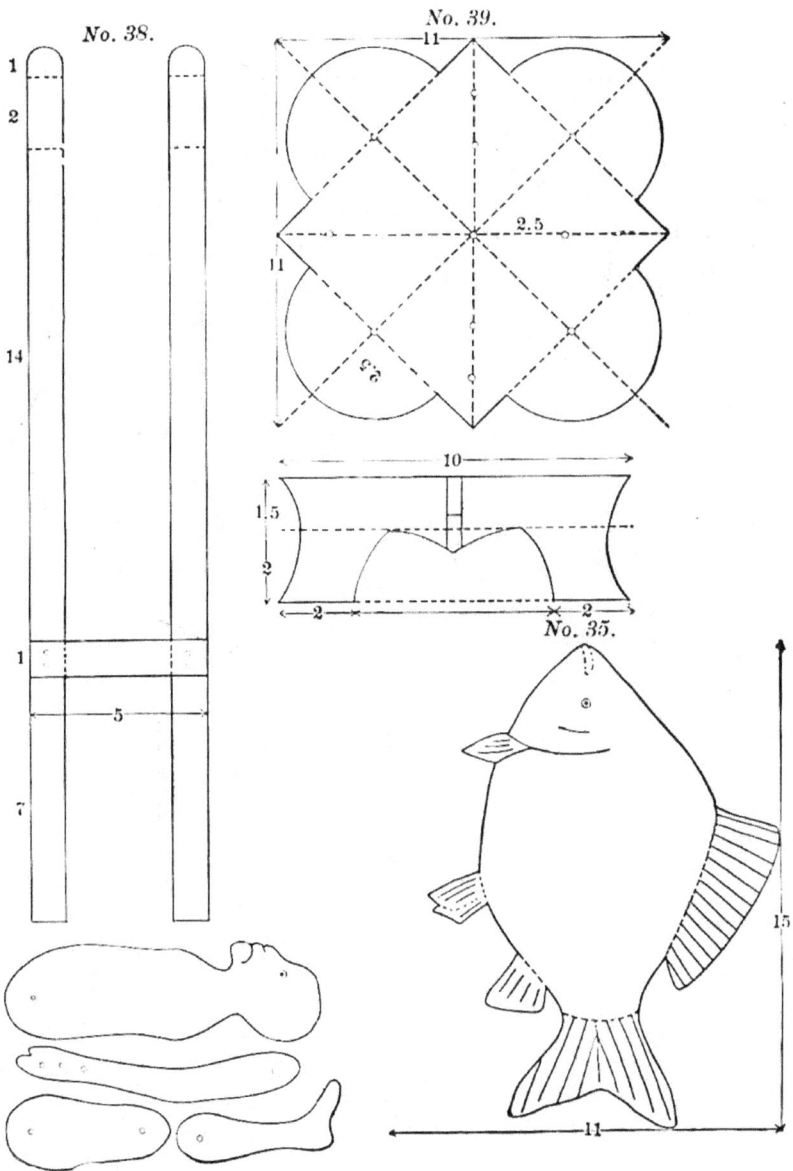

234 EVA RODHE'S MODEL SERIES

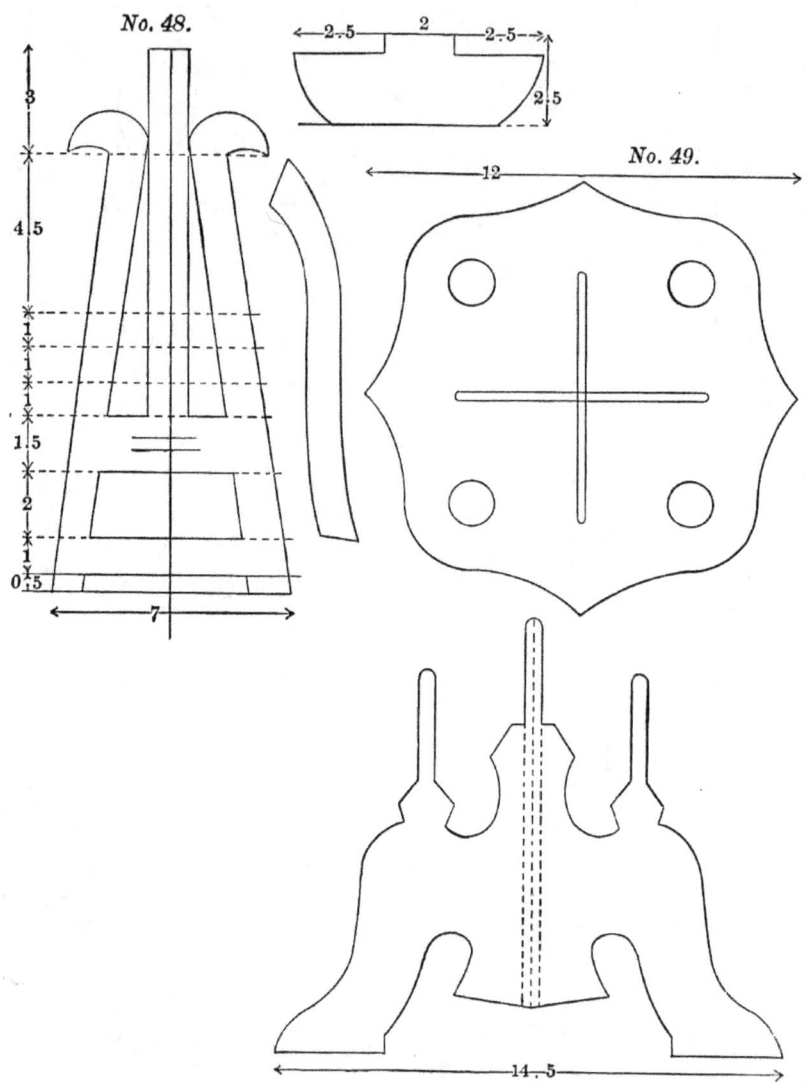

CHAPTER VI.

THE PROGRESS OF THE SLOYD IN THE ELEMENTARY PUBLIC SCHOOLS.

EXTENSION OF THE MOVEMENT IN EUROPE AND AMERICA.

IN 1870 the Sloyd was first taught in some of the primary schools of *Sweden*. Secretary of State Carlson, who at that time was also at the head of the ecclesiastical department, took a great interest in this question, and in 1877 he introduced a bill in the " Rikstag " (Congress), suggesting the adoption of a system of manual work for all the schools throughout the kingdom. As a direct consequence of his resolution, there appeared on the 11th of September of that year a royal mandate to the effect that to each school where the Sloyd had been taught a yearly stipend of 75 kroner ($21.00) should be paid. This was intended to meet the expense of the material to be used.[1] At this time a grant

---

[1] In Sweden, the average cost for wood used by one child is about 50 öre (14 cents) per year, the child working four hours a week and thirty-six weeks per year. In Stockholm,

of 1,500 kroner was paid each year to about 200 schools. However, the number of schools in which the Sloyd was taught increased so rapidly that in 1889 1,278 schools were receiving a subvention.

In 1876 a private normal Sloyd school was established in Karlstad, and in 1877 the government laid a proposition before the "Rikstag" to introduce the Sloyd in all of the public seminaries for teachers. At this time, as well as in 1880 (when the same question was moved by individual members), the "Rikstag" rejected the proposition, and it was not until 1887 that it was finally agreed to introduce the work in three public normal colleges—Karlstad, Lund, and Hernosand.

The "Landsting" (State Assemblies), the Hushållningssallskap (Industrial and Agricultural Associations), and several prominent private persons had worked zealously for this purpose. The Board of Aldermen of Stockholm introduced the Sloyd in their city schools in 1876. In Gothenburg, it had been introduced on a small scale in 1872, and five years later it was taught in all the schools.

the children work forty-one weeks, and seven and a half hours per week, and the average cost is one kroner (28 cents).

At first, the work consisted in teaching the elements of the various trades. In Stockholm, the transition to a regular educational manual training system took place in 1882, and in Gothenburg in 1887. In Gefle, Norköping, Linköping, Malmö, and various other towns, the educational Sloyd was taught from the outset. In the summer of 1887 a general meeting of Swedish teachers was held in Gothenburg. Universal satisfaction was expressed as to the results of this work. The academical authorities at Upsala and Lund have offered their students opportunities to do Sloyd work during certain hours of each day.

At the Nääs Sloyd Normal College, the method of instruction was originally worked out. Though the Sloyd is not a compulsory subject, there are in Sweden nearly 1,500 schools out of a possible 3,800, which have introduced the teaching of the " Nääs System." Since the Nääs was established in 1875, up to September, 1890, 1,349 teachers (1,060 of them being Swedes) have taken longer or shorter courses there.

In *Norway*, the " Storting " (Congress) of 1866 accepted the proposition of the government, and decided to give to every public school in which Sloyd was taught the sum of 80 kroner. The

Sloyd is taught in six public normal colleges, and also at the " Fredrikshåldssloyd-forenings Arbeidskole" (Fredrickshall Sloyd Association Working School). The instruction in all of the schools is in wood Sloyd, and the pupils who have had at least two hundred hours' instruction, and have done the required amount of work, receive a special mention of this fact in their graduation diplomas. According to the new Norwegian school law, the Sloyd is compulsory for boys of the age of eleven and twelve years, and optional for younger or older pupils.

By the statute of May, 1866, manual work was made obligatory for the country schools, and optional for the city schools, of *Finland*. In all teachers' seminaries, some manual work is at present being taught. In the public schools there are many lady teachers, and special courses have been arranged for them. The Finnish Hushållningssällskap encourage this work by giving yearly stipends and distributing models and drawings.

Educational Sloyd is of recent date in *Denmark*. In the autumn of 1885 a Danish Sloyd Union was formed, which assisted the establishment of a Teachers' Sloyd School in Copenhagen, and the introduction of this work into ten private high schools. It is generally in the high schools that the Sloyd has been carried on. In 1882 the " Kjöbenhavn-Husflidsforening " (Copenhagen Home Industrial Society) established a large Sloyd school for the children of the " Kommuneskolerne " (Public Schools).

In *Germany*, the " Deutscher Verein für erziehlische Knaben-handarbeit " (German Association for Educational Manual Work for Boys), which counts among its members some of the most prominent men in Germany, has been very successful in its propaganda in behalf of this movement, especially so when we take into consideration the conservatism that has always existed among German teachers. The governments of Prussia, Saxony, and Alsace-Lorraine have given both moral and material support to the system. Sloyd schools have been organized in a great many cities, and the German Government, which yearly calls a congress of the friends of Sloyd instruction, has founded a normal college in Leipzig.

In southern *Austria-Hungary* and in Bohemia, the movement has progressed very rapidly. The Sloyd has been introduced as an elective subject in the elementary schools. In Hungary this work dates back to 1870, when the minister of public instruction issued an order that instruction be given in at least one of the following subjects to all the boys of the primary schools; viz., agriculture, gardening, silk-cultivation, or Sloyd. In 1881 manual training was made compulsory in twenty-four state seminaries for teachers, and in the Normal College of Buda Pesth a three years' course was introduced.

In *Russia*, in the State Normal College of St. Petersburg and in several other teachers' seminaries of that city, since 1884, Sloyd has been taught. For lack of means, the work has progressed but slowly. In the Baltic provinces, much has been done to further the Swedish system.

The local governments of several of the cantons of *Switzerland* have, during the last seven years, supported private efforts for establishing Sloyd courses for teachers.

About four years ago, a commission of seventeen gentlemen from *Italy* was sent by the Italian Minister of Public Instruction to study the various manual training systems of Europe, and more especially the Swedish system of Sloyd instruction. Each member of this body took a course of Nääs, and has since then personally directed a class for teachers at home.

The law of March 28, 1882, passed by the Chamber of Deputies and the Senate in *France*, made manual training compulsory in all normal as well as public elementary schools. At that time, the " École normale speciale pour l'enseignement du travail manuel" (Special Teachers' Seminary for Manual Training Instruction) was established. Though this institution has been abolished, the study of this subject is carried on in about one hundred schools of Paris; the most prominent school is the " Rue Tournefort." At the international meeting in Havre, in 1885, it was stated that manual work was a necessary feature in every rational system of education.

The officers of the late liberal government of *Belgium* had already begun to make arrangements to introduce the Sloyd in normal and primary schools, when through the election of 1884 they were compelled to go out of office. The members of the present clerical ministerial party expressed their views in 1887, at which time the minister of public instruction stated that he had the greatest sympathy with the movement, and that the government would soon take active steps in the matter. As a result, courses for teachers were formed, all of which have been very largely attended. Two societies—" Société nationale du travail manuel" and "Le Sloyd"—have worked for its introduction in the public schools.

In *England*, a very active propaganda in favor of the adoption of the Swedish Sloyd has been going on. The most recent school laws are strongly in sympathy with the movement, and many school boards have made arrangements for the introduction of the system. A great many teachers have studied at Nääs. Several societies —"The Union of Sloyd Teachers Trained at Nääs" and the "Sloyd Association"—have been organized by those interested in the matter.

The new school law of *Scotland* is even stronger in its Sloyd clause than the English law.

American teachers have shown a deep interest in educational manual work. Various systems of manual training have been introduced in the school courses. In New York, Boston, San Francisco, and other places, the Swedish Sloyd has been introduced in private institutions.

Argentine Republic, *Chile*, and *Uruguay* have sent representatives to Nääs to study the Sloyd, with a view to adopting it in their primary schools.

The Government of *Japan* has the intention of introducing this work during the ensuing year.

Holland, *Spain*, and *Brazil* have likewise taken active steps in this direction.

www.ingramcontent.com/pod-product-compliance
Lightning Source LLC
Chambersburg PA
CBHW070542010526
44118CB00012B/1191